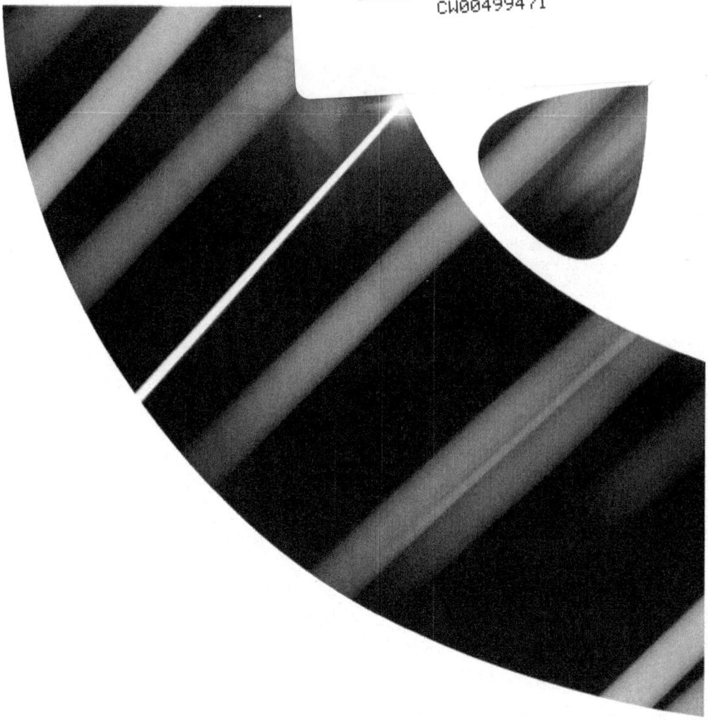

THE DATA-DRIVEN FUTURE:
UNLEASHING THE POWER OF AI AND EXPONENTIAL TECHNOLOGIES

By
Andrea Maria Cosentino, MSc and
Dr. Stylianos Kampakis PhD

IMPACT FUNDRY
Tesseract Academy

TABLE OF
CONTENT

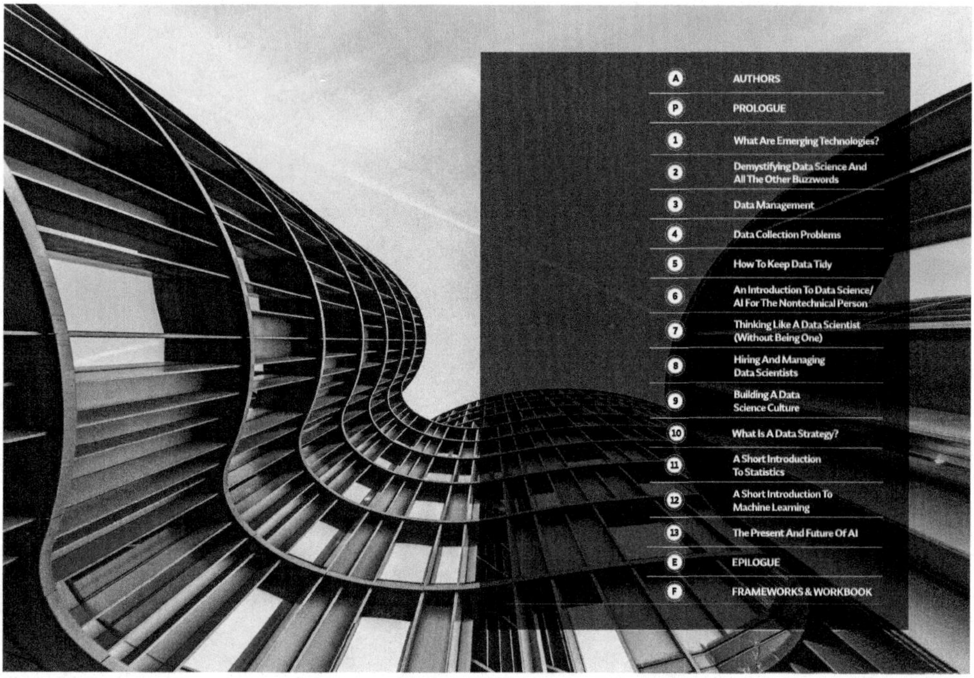

AUTH

HORS

ANDREA MARIA COSENTINO, MSc
CEO OF IMPACT FUNDRY

Andrea Maria Cosentino, MSc, is an Adjunct Professor of Digital Transformation & Entrepreneurship at Hult International Business School and ESCP Business School.

Andrea is the founder and CEO of Impact Fundry, a venture capital studio and strategic consulting boutique that accelerates start-ups, SMEs and corporate enterprise to enable growth and sustainable value creation. He is also a finance, digital transformation and entrepreneurship expert at the ESCP Business School and an advisor to several start-ups and accelerators, including

Barclays Rise and Level 39 in London. He lectures at various universities around the world and speaks at multiple conferences, with publications on LSE Tech Review, World Economic Forum, and MIT Tech Review. He contributed to the book The Internet of Value published by the Blockchain Center at UCL.

DR. STYLIANOS KAMPAKIS PhD
DATA SCIENTIST

Dr. Stylianos (Stelios) Kampakis is a data scientist living and working in London, UK. He holds a Ph.D. in Computer Science from the University College London and an MSc in Informatics from the University of Edinburgh. He also holds a degrees in Statistics, Cognitive Psychology, Economics, and Intelligent Systems. He is a member of the Royal Statistical Society and an honorary research fellow at the, UCL Centre for Blockchain Technologies.

He has many years of academic and industrial experience in all fields of data science like, statistical modeling, machine learning, classic AI, optimization, and more. Throughout his career, Stylianos performed a series of projects, from using deep learning methods to analyze data from mobile sensors, radar devices, and recommender systems to natural language processing for social-media data and predicting sports outcomes. He has also done work in econometrics, Bayesian modeling, forecasting, and research design. He also has many years of experience consulting for startups and scale-ups, having successfully worked with companies of all stages, some of which have raised millions of dollars in funding. He still provides, services in data science and blockchain as a partner in Electi Consulting.

He has many years of academic and industrial experience in all fields of data science like, statistical modeling, machine learning, classic AI, optimization, and more. Throughout his career, Stylianos performed a series of projects, from using deep learning methods to analyze data from mobile sensors, radar devices, and recommender systems to natural language processing for social-media data and predicting sports outcomes. He has also done work in econometrics, Bayesian modeling, forecasting, and research design. He also has many years of experience consulting for startups and scale-ups, having successfully worked with companies of all stages, some of which have raised millions of dollars in funding. He still provides, services in data science and blockchain as a partner in Electi Consulting.

In the academic domain, he is one of the foremost experts in sports analytics, having done his Ph.D. in machine learning for predicting football injuries. He has also published papers in neural networks, computational neuroscience, and cognitive science. Finally, he is also involved in blockchain research, supply chains, securitization of assets, and particularly in tokenomics. Stylianos is also very active in the area of data science education.

He founded The Tesseract Academy. The Tesseract Academy is a company whose mission is to help decision-makers understand deep technical topics such as machine learning and blockchain. He also teaches "Social Media Analytics" and "Quantitative Methods and Statistics with R" at the Cyprus International Institute of Management. He operates his own data science school in London called Datalyst.

Prologue

PROLOGUE

Prologue

The Data-Driven Future" is an engaging and accessible exploration of the intersection between Artificial Intelligence (AI), data, exponential technologies, and the strategies and business models that are shaping our world. Designed specifically for non-technical readers, this insightful book breaks down complex concepts and offers a clear understanding of how AI and data-driven approaches are revolutionizing industries and driving innovation.

Within these pages, you will embark on a journey that unveils the transformative potential of AI and its role as the driving force behind the data revolution. From machine learning algorithms to deep neural networks, the book provides a comprehensive overview of AI technologies and their practical applications in real-world scenarios.

"The Data-Driven Future" goes beyond technical jargon, ensuring that readers without technical backgrounds can grasp the key concepts. It illuminates the power of data as the lifeblood of modern enterprises, and how AI-driven strategies can unlock valuable insights, optimize operations, and deliver personalized customer experiences.

Drawing upon a rich tapestry of real-world examples and case studies, the book highlights how organizations across industries are leveraging AI and exponential technologies to gain a competitive edge. It offers practical frameworks and approaches for adopting AI and data-driven strategies, empowering readers to make informed decisions and build resilient business models.

While focusing on business strategies, the book also explores the ethical implications and societal impact of AI. It emphasizes the importance of responsible AI development and the need for ethical frameworks that align with societal values.

Written by industry experts and thought leaders in AI and data-driven innovation, "The Data-Driven Future" serves as a practical guide for executives, entrepreneurs, and professionals seeking to navigate the evolving landscape of AI and exponential technologies. It equips readers with the knowledge and tools necessary to embrace the data-driven future and unlock new opportunities for growth.

Whether you are a business leader, entrepreneur, or simply curious about the transformative power of AI and data, this book offers valuable insights in a language that is easily understood by non-technical readers. Prepare to embark on a captivating journey that demystifies AI, explores groundbreaking technologies, and unveils the limitless possibilities that lie ahead in the data-driven future.

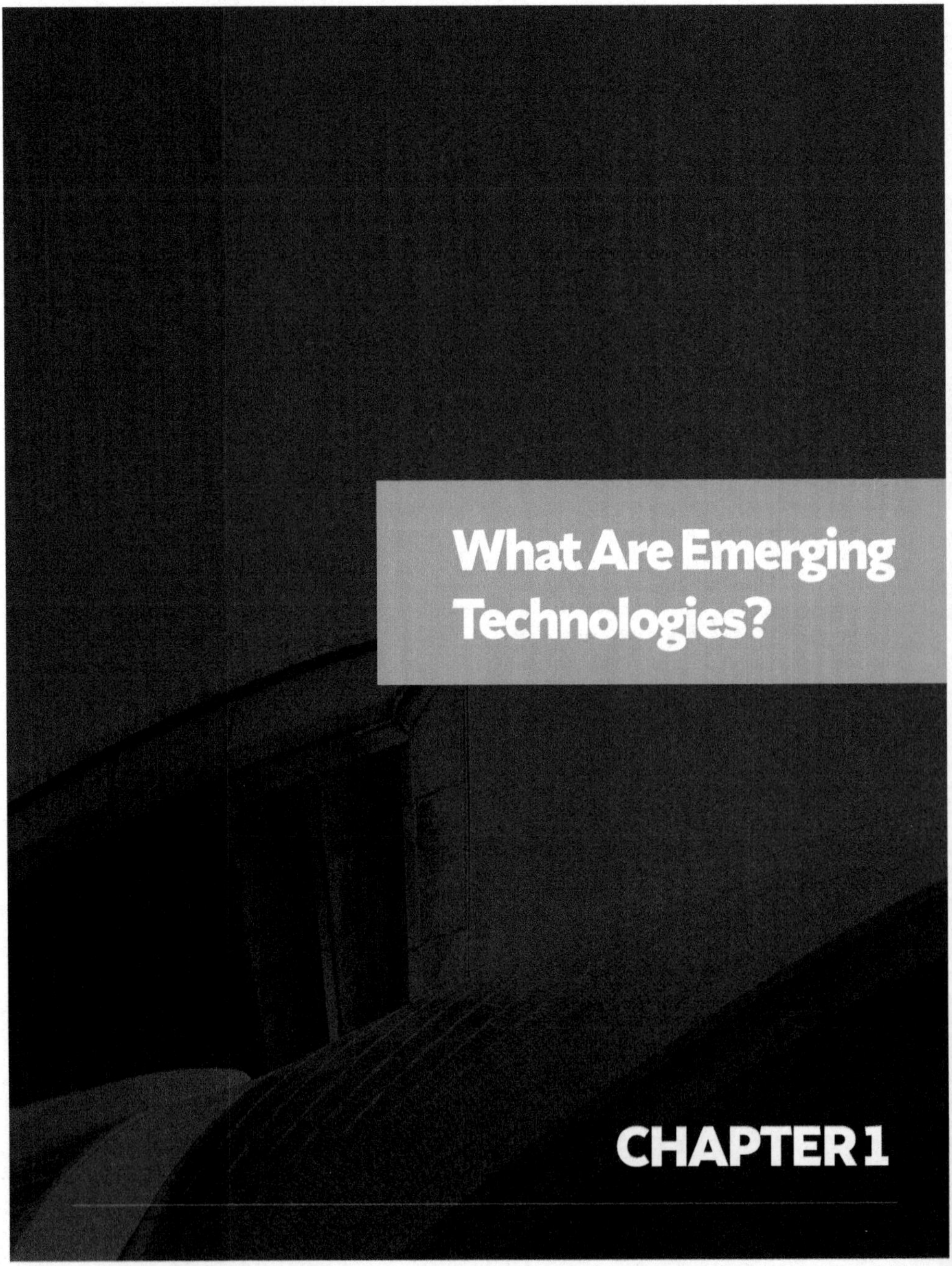

What Are Emerging Technologies?

CHAPTER 1

What Are Emerging Technologies?

We are in the midst of what many are calling the "Fourth Industrial Revolution." With so many emerging technologies that are changing our society, it's an accurate description. And, like the three previous industrial revolutions, our world will evolve to a completely new level.

But what are emerging technologies?

Emerging technologies represent any technology with massive potential that hasn't been fully realized. It can be an old or new tech. The key is that it can completely change society, either through its development or application. Gene therapy is an example of an older technology that can still be classed as emerging tech. Developed in the early 1990s, gene therapy still has a lot of potential that hasn't been explored.

More recent innovations that are classed as emerging technologies include artificial intelligence (AI)/data science, blockchain, the "Internet of things" (IoT), 3D printing, 5G, quantum computing, and robotics (Figure 1.1). These are all technologies that are still in their infancy. Yet, they have already significantly changed the world we live in. As these technologies evolve, the degree of change will amplify until we reach a point where society will be completely different from even a few years ago. A quick look at history proves that this is exactly what will happen.

The History of Technological Disruption

Humanity's history is peppered with technological disruption. Throughout our existence, technology has played a significant role in our society.

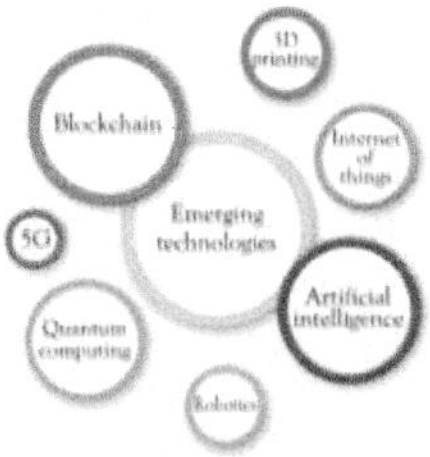

Figure 1.1 Emerging technologies

From humanity's invention of the wheel and the development of agriculture to the harnessing of electricity and the invention of computers, many of our significant leaps of societal progress can be attributed to technological progress.

Take the First Industrial Revolution. Starting around 1760, it introduced mechanical production, thanks to the invention of the steam engine. Suddenly, people didn't have to do everything by hand. Steam-powered machines could do a lot of the hard work—they could also do it faster and often better.

People could also travel faster and more easily, thanks to steamships and trains, basically making the world a smaller place. It also saw the rise of the middle class.

Then came the Second Industrial Revolution, where things such as petrol engines, chemical fertilizers, and airplanes once again changed the world. This was also the age of mass production, making it easier for people to get what they needed. And since people always follow employment, there was a significant migration of the population from rural to urban centers. How people lived also changed. Things such as electric lighting, the radio, and the telephone transformed society.

The Third Industrial Revolution was dubbed the Digital Revolution and started in the 1950s. It saw the rise of semiconductors, personal computing, and the Internet.

The shift from analog to digital changed the world in ways no one could have expected. Every industry was affected, including global communication, energy, and manufacturing.

Think of mobile phones. They completely changed society. Before mobile phones, if something happened and you weren't in reach of a telephone (like getting a flat tire in the middle of nowhere), one had to hope someone would come along who could help.

Now? All one has to do is whip their phone out and call for assistance. Of course, that's if the car itself hasn't already alerted the service provider of the problem. Then again, that is IoT, so we're getting a bit
ahead of ourselves.

Nevertheless, the past two decades alone have seen society change massively to what it once was. And all that is due to technological progress, which leads us to the Fourth Industrial Revolution.

The Fourth Industrial Revolution: Sci-Fi Coming to Reality

One thing that won't change is the danger of failing to adapt. Businesses that aren't prepared to change and avoid adopting new tech will disappear.

Historically, those that didn't adopt steam engines and stuck to their ways couldn't compete. The same happened to companies that didn't take advantage of the developments of the Second and Third Industrial Revolutions.

Likewise, businesses that do not evolve and get left behind in the race for tech adoption will experience the same fate, especially since we live in a consumer-driven world where the consumer is becoming increasingly tech-savvy, and expectations have skyrocketed.

Let's take a quick look at some of the emerging technologies driving the Fourth Industrial Revolution.

What Are Emerging Technologies?

AI/Data Science

The business world has evolved, moving past making decisions based on people's digestive systems. Big Data is now primarily driving decision-making.

However, Big Data is getting bigger every day, which makes analysis more challenging. And that is where AI comes in. Without AI systems to analyze all that data, companies would be stuck with a slew of information that, in essence, would be useless. And without insights derived from the raw data, decisions would continue to be as gut-based as ever.

AI isn't just being used to provide better insights, either, as machine learning (ML) solutions are increasingly being used in manufacturing and industrial settings to make decisions. From adjusting the working parameters of a machine on a production line to scheduling maintenance for a piece of equipment in an industrial facility to running simulations on a digital twin to identify failure points, ML algorithms are becoming an increasingly important part of Industry 4.0.

In the context of Industry 4.0, one of the most significant applications of AI and ML is in managing market demand.

Anticipating future market demand typically involves analyzing historical data. Manufacturers will achieve much higher levels of innovation by leveraging the power of AI and ML tools.

An ML algorithm can look at things such as weather patterns, major events, socioeconomic issues, and consumer behavior to make assessments of market demand for products before they hit the production line.

The ML algorithm can then use this analysis to optimize everything from staffing to inventory to raw material purchasing to ensure optimal performance. As these ML tools become more widespread, they will have a game-changing impact on the manufacturing industry.

Blockchain

Blockchain has already started to change retail, government, banking, and many more sectors. By decentralizing systems, blockchain eliminates many inefficiencies and, more importantly, creates never-before-seen transparency.

Unsurprisingly, blockchain is driving change simply by existing. For example, even if traditional financial organizations haven't jumped on the blockchain bandwagon, they've had to improve their services to remain competitive.

In terms of Industry 4.0, blockchain technologies have transformative potential in a range of areas. One example is supply chain management, where blockchain technologies can improve transparency, reduce risks, and cut processes that traditionally take days or weeks down to minutes or hours.

By utilizing blockchain technologies, products can be monitored in real-time as they move through the supply chain. There is no risk of someone trying to alter a completion or delivery date. Delays in communication can also be minimized as everyone in the supply chain has access to the same information immediately. This reduces the need for ineffective and inefficient communication methods such as e-mail.

Financial transactions in the supply chain can also be streamlined with the additional benefit of maximum transparency. Again, this can help to eliminate delays caused by communication inefficiencies and human error.

Other applications for the blockchain in the factory of the future include:

- Quality control—where each component, manufacturing process, and assembly process is stored in the blockchain along with multiple other data points, from temperatures to humidity levels to dates and more.
- Traceability—traceability is a key process in many industries, and it is becoming more important, even when regulations don't require it. Blockchain offers a decentralized and highly efficient method of ensuring product traceability throughout the full product life cycle.
- Compliance—compliance is a major consideration in industries such as pharmaceuticals and food production, and companies are always looking for ways to streamline their compliance processes. New blockchain technologies have the potential to achieve these efficiency savings.

Fraud prevention—product fraud is a major issue for a range of industries, from clothing manufacturers to pharmaceuticals. The un-editable nature of blockchain technologies makes them ideally suited for the creation of new fraud prevention tools to help protect the manufacturing sector.

IoT

The IoT is turning sci-fi into reality. "Smart" equipment that transfers data without human input is revolutionizing how we do everything.

From heart monitor implants keeping people healthy to refrigerators that can order groceries, IoT is changing how we live and do business.

Another example of how IoT technologies are transforming business in the Industry 4.0 era is R&D and new product development. In the past, product development teams would be forced to use incomplete and often inaccurate data, as well as subjective opinions, to determine the focus for future development. With the IoT, product developers can get real-time information on exactly how people are using products, as well as on how well those products are performing. This will lead to a much more user-first approach

to product development across all industries.
There is also the Industrial Internet of Things (IIoT). It is an extension of the IoT as it focuses on the technologies that apply to the industrial and manufacturing environments. As with the IoT, the IIoT is about connecting a range of different devices, equipment, and machines in an industrial setting. However, where the IoT is making the biggest impact is in narrowing the gap between IT (information technology) and OT (operational technology).

Traditionally in the manufacturing sector, IT and OT were completely separate, with little connectivity or integration. So, for example, Customer Relationship Management (CRM), accounting, and sales apps that are part of IT would have no integration with the equipment, systems, and platforms that produce the products on the factory floor.
IIoT technologies are playing an important role in facilitating the integration of IT and IIoT, improving productivity, efficiency, and oversight in manufacturing organizations.

3D Printing
3D printing has already disrupted multiple industries. In health care, medical professionals are printing prosthetics and replicas of bones, organs, and blood vessels, all tailored to a specific patient.

It can also help reduce waste, build homes for everyone, provide clothing, feed the homeless, and more.
Essentially, this is a technology that, when combined with all the other emerging tech, can eventually lead us to make whatever we need with the push of a button, from vehicles to food.
Even simple applications are being transformed by 3D printing, such as producing a prototype of a product currently being developed. 3D-printed prototypes can be produced in a fraction of the time and at a fraction of the cost with less costly equipment. This is just one other example of how 3D printing is a game-changer.

5G Technology
5G is already taking the world by storm as it offers faster speeds, more capacity, and reduced latency for mobile networks. In other words, more data can be transferred at much higher speeds, which will drive significant change in our society.
For example, it could help improve public safety in emergencies. The ability to handle higher volumes of high-quality video means that authorities can more effectively analyze emergencies, thereby leading to more effective responses.
5G technology is also a key driver of IoT, plus it enables highly innovative edge computing solutions.
5G technology also means that data can also be processed at the edge, improving performance.

There are multiple reasons why 5G is important to Industry 4.0. First, 5G enables faster communication between systems, platforms, and equipment. This reduces latency to a point that is close to wired connections, it helps to optimize production processes where physical connections are impractical.

5G technologies also make it possible to transmit critical communications reliably and in real-time. This was not possible previously when the only option was 4G technologies. Not only does the reliability, speed, and low latency of 5G have productivity implications but also safety benefits.

Quantum Computing

Quantum computers will be able to solve many computationally impossible problems, which will revolutionize many industries.

For example, quantum computing can help scientists discover and develop new drugs much faster. At the same time, in finances, these systems can provide better analytics and help improve trading, data speed, and transactions.

While this technology is in its infancy, quantum computing has usage applications across a wide range of areas. Enhancing risk management is one example, as well as enabling manufacturers to achieve faster and more customer-centric production. Business strategies such as mass customization are set to become the norm as quantum computing develops further.

Quantum computing will also see the introduction of sensors that are smaller and more sensitive. This will not only have benefits for the products that manufacturing companies produce but it will also help to improve manufacturing processes, given the importance of sensors in developing smart factories.

Metrology is another area of manufacturing in which quantum computing is predicted to have a significant impact. For many manufacturers, metrology is an essential driver for quality assurance and, by extension, optimizing manufacturing processes.

Metrology technologies and solutions that utilize quantum computing will take the field to another level. It will provide manufacturing organizations with new data and insights and achieve greater levels of accurate measurement and process repeatability.

Robotics

Progress in robotics is accelerating, and we've already seen automation implemented in the manufacturing industry, leading to increased efficiencies. But robotics continues to evolve and, as AI and ML progress, it won't be long before robots can take over many more of the jobs that humans have to do now.

As robots become more prevalent, productivity rises, and the economy will grow. However, we will also see a shift in society as the types of jobs humans do will change. One area of robotics, rapidly advancing in the Industry 4.0 era, is the development of robotic solutions that work alongside people.

This type of equipment is often referred to as Cobots. From autonomous vehicles to manufacturing and assembly lines, the efficiency gains that can be made with Cobots and similar technologies are significant.

Then there is the concept of the lights-out factory, where robots are responsible for 100 percent of manufacturing and assembly processes, and are able to operate 24 hours a day, 7 days a week. They can do this without taking holidays, without making mistakes, and without getting tired or sick. We are still some distance away from this concept becoming a reality on anything like a widespread basis, and there are some who believe it won't be feasible. However, the lights out factory is the general direction of travel.

We are still some distance away from this concept becoming a reality on anything like a widespread basis, and some believe it won't be feasible. However, the lights-out factory is the general direction of travel.

There are many reasons for this, and advances in robotic technologies are high-up on that list. Other, more traditional considerations are great too. The significance of having access to labor cannot be overlooked. In many industries, upgrading production lines with robots isn't about replacing people. Instead, it is about changing a process because they find it increasingly difficult to recruit and train the right skills.

Summary

The Fourth Industrial Revolution is happening right now. This revolution is being driven by multiple technologies which disrupt the world individually. However, when one combines these technologies, they facilitate even greater levels of change.

Robotics is an excellent example. We started with robots that had to be programmed to perform the tiniest action. When we needed them to do something different, the code had to be changed. They certainly couldn't learn or think on their own. But AI and ML are changing that.

This book will focus on two of the most prominent emerging technologies: AI/Data Science, and Blockchain. We'll look at what these emerging technologies are, and how they're changing the world.

What Are Emerging Technologies?

Our focus areas are AI/Data Science and Blockchain since these technologies offer the most value compared to others and have gained tremendous popularity in recent times.

5G technology is undoubtedly a game-changer in the world of telecommunications, and the amount of data generated by IoT is just massive. However, to extract the most value from these advancements, we need to leverage data science techniques. Moreover, by combining the power of these technologies with blockchain, we can unlock even more potential for innovative applications. Also, robotics can be seen as an application of AI, which is related to data science. Therefore, these two technologies are what a decision-maker needs to know about right now. We'll also look at why businesses need to adopt these technologies to remain competitive. After all, history proves that lagging in tech adoption will only lead to obscurity.

Key Takeaways

- The term "emerging technologies" refers to a group of technological advancements that define Industry 4.0.
- The key technologies of this revolution are AI/data science and blockchain.

Demystifying Data Science And All The Other Buzzwords

CHAPTER 2

Demystifying Data Science And All The Other Buzzwords

In the business world, data has become a big thing. You hear all sorts of buzz- words being thrown around left, right, and center. Things like big data, artificial intelligence, machine learning, data mining, deep learning, and so on. This can get confusing, leaving you paralyzed as to what is the best technology to use and under what circumstances. In this chapter, we are going to demystify all these buzzwords, by taking a short stroll through the history of data science. You will understand how the history of data analysis gave birth to different schools of thought and disciplines, which have now all come together under the umbrella of the term data science.

What Is Data Science?

In 2017, we generated more data than we did over the previous 5000 years of our history.1 That's a lot of data. And it's not surprising. Every device we own generates data, and all our interactions with said devices generate even more data. So, you take a picture with your smartphone? You've generated data. You read the news on your tablet? You're generating data. You listen to a podcast on your laptop? You're generating data. You go on Facebook to update your status? You've generated data.

You get the point. There's a good chance that the only thing we do that doesn't generate data is breathe, but even that is debatable considering all the wearable devices that are available and which can track everything from heart rate to calories burned.

What happens to all this data? It must have some use or things wouldn't be set up so that we generate it in the first place.

At the moment, some of it does and some of it doesn't. In fact, some studies have discovered that less than 0.5% of data is being analyzed and turned into actionable insights.3 But more on that later. The important thing is that all data can be used. We just need to figure out better ways of doing so.

And this is where data science comes in. There are many definitions of data science. One such definition is:
Data science is a "concept to unify statistics, data analysis, machine learning and their related methods" in order to "understand and analyze actual phenomena" with data.4

Okay, so those are a lot of big and fancy words, which can get confusing. Let's boil it down to the simplest definition:

Data science is about using data to do useful stuff.
Short and to the point. That's exactly what data science is all about.

The methods we use are important, of course, but the essence of this discipline is that it allows us to take data and transform it so we can use it to do useful things.

For example, let's say someone visits a doctor because they are short of breath. They are experiencing heartburn and they have chest pains. The doctor will run the basic tests, including measuring blood pressure, but nothing seems out of the ordinary.

Since the patient is overweight, the doctor immediately assumes the symptoms are caused by the patient's size and recommends a healthier diet and exercise. Three months later, the same patient is brought into the emergency room and ends up dying on the table because of a heart defect.

This might sound like an episode on your favorite medical show, that is, a work of fiction, but it happens much more often than you might think. In fact, in the United States, 5% of patients are misdiagnosed, while misdiagnosis cost the United Kingdom over £197 million in the 2014/2015 fiscal year. However, this situation can be avoided thanks to data science. The analysis of similar cases reveals that the symptoms our patient exhibited aren't just caused by obesity but also by some cardiovascular conditions.

Having access to systems that can analyze data and compare it with new data inputs could have helped the doctor identify the problem sooner without relying solely on their own personal experience and knowledge.
So, data science can be used to save lives, among many other applications, which is pretty useful.

Data Science Is Multidisciplinary
Data science involves multiple disciplines, which is why finding someone with the necessary skills to be a data scientist can be difficult.
Thus, data science involves everything from statistics and pattern recognition to business analysis and communication. It requires creative thinking as much as it requires analytical thinking.6

So, data science involves discovering which data is useful as well as effective ways of managing it. It also requires determining how the data should be processed and what types of insights can be garnered from the massive amounts of data available.

Data science requires knowledge of programming and computing, but also visualization so that the insights can be presented in a way that everyone can understand.

Furthermore, business acumen is also a necessity because while data science can be applied to any field of business, it is critical to know what types of answers the business needs and how to present said insights so leadership can understand them.

Core Fields of Data Science

Data science has three core fields, namely, artificial intelligence, machine learning, and statistics.

Artificial intelligence is all about replicating human brain function in a machine. The primary functions that AI should perform are logical reasoning, self-correction, and learning. While it has a wide range of applications, it is also a highly complicated technology because to make machines smart, a lot of data and computing power is required.

Machine learning refers to a computer's ability to learn and improve beyond the scope of its programming. Thus, it relies on creating algorithms that are capable of learning from the data they are given. They are also designed to garner insights and then make forecasts regarding data they haven't previously analyzed.

There are three approaches to machine learning, namely, supervised, unsupervised, and reinforcement learning, plus some subfields (such as semi-supervised learning). Here, we will be talking only about supervised and unsupervised learning, since this is what is mainly used in business.

Let's say you want to sort all your photographs based on content. In supervised learning, you would provide the computer with labeled examples. So, you'd give it a picture of a dog and label it animal. Then you'd feed it a picture of a person and label it human. The machine will then sort all the remaining pictures.
In unsupervised learning, you'd just give the machine all the photos and let it figure out the different characteristics and organize your photos.

In reinforcement learning, the machine learns based on errors and rewards. Thus, the machine analyzes its actions and their results. A good example of reinforcement learning is a rat in a maze that needs to navigate its way to a piece of cheese. The learning process that helps the rat achieve this can be implemented in a machine through reinforcement learning. This is one of the most esoteric types of machine learning.
Statistics is an essential tool in the arsenal of any data scientist because it helps develop and study methods to collect, analyze, interpret, and present data. The numerous methodologies it uses enable data scientists to

- Design experiments and interpret results to improve product decision-making
- Build signal-predicting models
- Transform data into insights
- Understand engagement, conversions, retention, leads, and more

- Make intelligent estimations
- Use data to tell the story

Let's take a closer look at all three.

Artificial Intelligence: A Little History

In 1954, the field of AI research came into being at a workshop at Dartmouth College. There, the attendees discussed topics that would influence the field for years to come.

As we've already explained, the goal of artificial intelligence is to create a "thinking machine," that is, one that emulates human brain function. To do this, of course, one needs to understand the human mind, which is why AI is closely related to the field of cognitive science. Cognitive science involves studying the human mind and its processes, including intelligence and behavior. Memory, language, perception, attention, emotion, and reasoning are all studied, and to gain greater understanding of these faculties, scientists borrow from other fields, including

- Linguistics
- Psychology
- Philosophy
- Neuroscience
- Anthropology
- Artificial intelligence

Artificial intelligence played a key part in the development of cognitive science, and there was a large interplay between cognitive psychology and AI. The understanding of human cognition helped us improve our understanding of how to transfer this inside machines. Vice versa, the computational theory of the mind was one of the dominant paradigms in cognitive science. According to this theory, the mind works like a computer, with processes and limited memory. While this is now considered outdated, it drove research for decades.

The AI Dream

It all started with a grand vision. Marvin Minsky, the head of the artificial laboratory at MIT who was considered the father of AI, stated that "artificial intelligence is the science of making machines do things that would require intelligence if done by men."8

In other words, the dream was to create an intelligent machine. So, how would one go about doing it? First, we start with intuition, that is, the human's distinct ability for logical reasoning. Logical reasoning is, essentially, the capacity to reason based on various premises to reach a conclusion that has logical certainty. For example:

If all men are mortal, and Socrates is a man, then Socrates is mortal.

Or:
If it's raining outside and I don't have an umbrella, I will get wet if I go out.
To translate this logical deduction ability to a machine, a rule-based or symbolic approach is used. This involves humans constructing a system of rules with which the computer is programmed. Using these rules, reasoning algorithms are capable of deriving logical conclusions.

A good example is MYCIN,9 which was an early successful working system based on reasoning algorithms. It was used to diagnose infections and determine the type of bacteria that was causing the problem. It was never used in a clinical setting but is an excellent example of an expert system and a predecessor to machine learning.

The system was developed in the 1970s at Stanford University and had approximately 600 rules.10 Users were required to provide answers to various questions and the program would then provide a list of potential bacteria that could be causing the problem, sorted from high to low probability. It would also provide its confidence in the probability of each diagnosis as well as how it came to the conclusion. Finally, it would provide the recommended course of treatment.

It had a 69% accuracy rate, and it was claimed that the program was more effective than junior doctors and on the same level as some experts.11

The program was created by interviewing a large number of experts who provided their expertise and experience. It used rules of the IF (condition)THEN (conclusion) form. For example, IF (sneezing and coughing or head- ache) THEN (flu).

One limitation the program had was computing power. It took approximately 30 minutes to go through the system, which was too much wasted time in a real-world clinical setting.
Another issue was also raised, namely, that of ethics and legal issues. Thus, the question arose of who would be held responsible of the program made the wrong diagnosis or recommended the wrong treatment.

Though it was never used, MYCIN still had a very important role in bringing us to where we are today as it was one of the early successes of AI, proving what is possible and strengthening.

Automated Planning
Planning is a vital component of rational behavior. Automated planning and scheduling is an area of artificial intelligence that involves the creation of a system that is capable of selecting and organizing actions to achieve a certain outcome.
An example is the Missionaries and Cannibals problem,12 which is a classic AI puzzle. It is defined as follows:

On one bank of a river are three missionaries and three cannibals. They all wish to cross to the other side of the river. There is one boat available that can hold up to two people. However, if the cannibals ever outnumber the missionaries on either of the river's banks, the missionaries will get eaten.
How can the boat be used to safely carry all the missionaries and cannibals across the river?
It's a little gruesome and might also seem trivial, but a similar approach can be used for schedule planning.

Other similar problems are the towers of Hanoi13 and the travelling salesman problem. The travelling salesman problem is a legendary benchmark in optimization, where the objective is to find a path for a salesman to go across all the cities in a country (or some other geographical regions). This path should never go through the same city twice, and at the same time it should be as short as possible. It is easy to see how this relates to vehicle routing in real life. In Figure 1-1, you can see an example of the travelling salesman for all major cities in Germany.

Fig 2.1 Example of the travelling salesman problem

Essentially, what the computer does is analyze each possibility, discarding the one that doesn't fulfill the parameters while presenting all the options that do.

The AI Winters

Artificial intelligence would likely be much further along now were it not for the "winters" it experienced. The term AI winter refers to periods when interest in artificial intelligence was diminished, and, as a result, funding was limited.

In 1967, Marvin Minsky predicted that "within a generation the problem of creating 'artificial intelligence' will be substantially solved." However, by 1982, he admitted that "the AI problem is one of the hardest science has ever undertaken."14

The first major AI winter started in 1974 and ended in 1980, while the second one started in 1987 and ended in 1993. There were other smaller issues, such as

- 1966—The failure of machine translation
- 1970—The abandonment of connectionism
- 1971-1975—DARPA's frustration with the Speech Understanding Research program at Carnegie Mellon University
- 1973—The large decrease in AI research in the United Kingdom in response to the Lighthill report
- 1973-1974—DARPA's cutbacks to academic AI research in general
- 1987—The collapse of the Lisp machine market
- 1988—The cancellation of new spending on AI by the Strategic Computing Initiative
- 1993—Expert systems slowly reaching the bottom
- 1990s—The quiet disappearance of the fifth-generation computer project's original goals

The first winter was caused, in large part, by three major elements. First, it was the Lighthill report, in which professor Sir James Lighthill concluded that other sciences could do everything being done in AI, implying that many of the most successful AI algorithms would be incapable of solving real-world problems.15

Though contested, the report still resulted in the complete shutdown of AI research in the United Kingdom, with only a few universities continuing the research. The result was funding cuts for this research all across Europe.16 In 1969, the Mansfield Amendment was passed in the United States, requiring DARPA to fund research that had a clear mission rather than basic projects with no clear direction. Essentially, researchers had to prove their projects would quickly produce technology that would be useful to the military.

In concert with Lighthill's report, which was used as proof that AI research was unlikely to provide anything useful in the foreseeable future, DARPA stopped funding this type of research. By 1974, funding for AI was virtually impossible to find.17 Another issue was the Speech Understanding Research program at Carnegie Mellon. DARPA wanted a system that could respond to spoken commands from a pilot, and while the team had developed a system that understood spoken English, the words had to be spoken in a certain order.

DARPA felt they had been misled and cancelled the grant in 1974.18 Interestingly enough, by 2001 the speech recognition market reached $4 billion and used the technology the team from

Carnegie Mellon developed.19

In 1980, the commercial success of expert systems rekindled interest in the field of AI. By 1985, over a billion dollars was being spent on AI and an industry developed to support the field. Specialized computers dubbed Lispmachines were built to better process the programming language that was preferred for AI.

Unfortunately, the Lisp machine market collapsed because companies like Sun Microsystems developed more efficient alternatives. These general workstations had much better performance, which Lisp machines were incapable of matching. This led to the second AI winter.

What We Learned from AI Research

Despite all the issues, research into artificial intelligence discovered many beneficial things. For example, if it weren't for AI research, we would not have algorithms that work with logical rules.

An early example of such an algorithm was the Prolog language. One of the first logic-based programming languages, it's still one of the most popular even today. It has been used to prove theorems, in expert systems, in type inference, and for automated planning.

And that's another area where AI has helped us. Automated planning and scheduling, which is used to drive things like automated robots in manufacturing, would not exist otherwise. Neither would expert systems or knowledge representation.

Of course, all these things have evolved significantly since then, and we are getting closer and closer to creating true AI, but we still have a long way to go before we have a truly intelligent machine.

Another interesting aspect is that cognitive science borrows from AI as much as the reverse is true. The desire to develop a smart machine that can think like a human required a better understanding of the human mind. This led to research into memory, perception, and much more.

The Next Step: Enter Machine Learning

As a term, machine learning was coined by Arthur Samuel, who was a pioneer in computer gaming and AI, in 1959 while working at IBM.20

He defined it as follows:

Machine learning is about giving computers the ability to learn without being explicitly programmed.

A rift caused by the focus on logical, knowledge-based approaches developed between machine learning and AI. By the 1980s, expert systems dominated AI, and statistics was no longer of interest.

Machine learning was then reorganized as a separate field and began to gain serious traction in the 1990s. Instead of focusing on creating artificial intelligence, machine learning shifted its approach and concentrated on solving more practical problems. Thus, instead of employing the symbolic methodologies so prevalent in AI, it began to employ models taken from statistics and probability theory.

While machine learning as a concept is a subfield of artificial intelligence, its approach was practically opposite to research that had been done so far.21

Thus, "classic AI" or "good-old-fashioned AI" took a ruled-based, top-down approach. Essentially, it meant giving computers rules that they had to follow to reach the desired outcome. The problem with this approach is that it requires a lot of human input.

The designer of the system must be able to predict every possibility and create a set of rules for it. Furthermore, uncertainty is not easily handled because the machine thinks in an IF/THEN pattern.

Unfortunately, the world isn't always so clear-cut. In the real world, IF (EVENT A) takes place, THEN (ACTION B) isn't always the solution. For example, IF (SUNNY) doesn't always result in

THEN (WEAR LIGHT CLOTHING). It could be winter out and you could need a heavy coat. Furthermore, the system only knows to provide this answer because it's been told what to do.

Machine learning, on the other hand, takes a bottom-up, data-driven approach.

So, instead of programming a computer with rules it must follow, machine learning uses data to teach the computer what to do. There is very little human input involved, other than providing the data. This allows the machine to handle uncertainty more naturally, making it a more effective approach since the world is fundamentally more probabilistic than certain.

With our rain analogy, machine learning would work a little like this. The system is fed a ton of data and it analyzes what happens when there is a certain type of weather. So, when it's sunny, it sees people going out in both light and heavy clothing. It learns even more when it makes the connection that tem-perature also matters. Essentially, it recognizes patterns: sun + cold temperature = warmer clothing. The machine does this on its own by analyzing and learning from data it has been given.

The problem with machine learning for a while was that it required a lot of data to work effectively.
Thankfully, with technological progress like the development of the Internet and cheap storage, the data-driven approach has become more popular. Not only is it more effective, but it's also more feasible from an economic and technological viewpoint too.

The Problem with Machine Learning

Of course, machine learning has its drawbacks, just like anything else. First of all, machine learning can't handle logic rules directly, and how we can integrate machine learning with reasoning is an open question. Let's take gravity as an example. Machine learning can come to the conclusion that there is a 0.99 probability of an object falling if you let it go. This, however, is based on past data and it cannot make the logical leap that "any" object will fall if you let it go because of gravity. It can give probabilities based on past events, but it cannot come to the conclusion: IF (GRAVITY) THEN (OBJECT FALL). This logical leap is something that even babies can do, demonstrating that while machine learning can be very powerful, it is far from intelligent the way the inventors of AI envisioned it.

Another issue is that machine learning isn't all that transparent. Most algorithms are a "black box," with input going in on one side and the results being spat out on the other side. However, we don't see what's happening inside the box. Think of Google's famous search algorithm. We know we enter a search string and we get the "most" relevant results, but we don't see how that happens.

Interpretable machine learning is now a very active field of investigation.22

Deep Learning

Deep learning is the field of research that studies deep neural networks, which
is a neural network with multiple layers. A neural network will have one or two layers, whereas deep neural networks have many more (Figure 2-2).

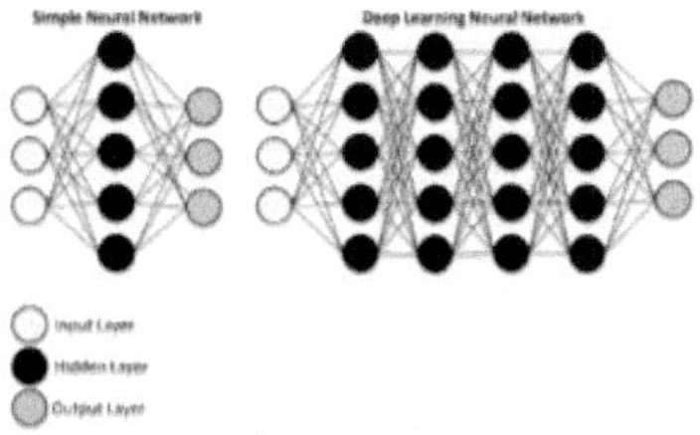

Fig 2-2 Example of a regular neural network vs. a deep neural break

Geoffrey Hinton, a British cognitive psychologist and computer scientist who is regarded as the "Godfather of Deep Learning," discovered it was impossible to get his research into neural networks published, so he had to devise a new term that was "cooler."23

Neural networks consist of neurons and the pathways that connect them in the human brain. Since the brain is the most powerful computing machine known to man, it makes sense to attempt to emulate its architecture, which led to the creation of artificial neural networks.

Neural networks have traditionally consisted of three layers: an input layer, a middle layer, and an output layer. The middle layer is what provided the neural networks with the power to perform non-linear computations and turned them into powerful learning machines.

The idea behind deep learning had been around for decades.24 However, it was believed that adding more layers was not really useful. Furthermore, it was difficult to train these networks.

Deep learning takes advantage of artificial neural networks to enable machines to learn faster, more accurately, and at scale. Thus, it is used to help develop solutions to many issues that were previously unsolvable, such as speech recognition, computer vision, and natural language processing.

For example, applications like Siri or Cortana are able to understand what you want thanks to deep learning. Image recognition, for example, can help you find furniture you see in the real world. Just take a picture of the piece and the app will find it online for you.

Thanks to deep learning, machines can also identify different subjects in a photo—like differentiating between a human, a horse, a cat, and a dog. It can also be used to automatically color photos and, more recently, to automatically remove the background of a photo, which many designers will be extremely grateful for.

It is also being used to generate text automatically. In other words, thanks to deep learning, your computer can listen to what you're saying and turn your words into text.

Basically, deep learning can do a lot of really cool stuff!

But how does it do that and why it works so well? The multiple layers of a deep neural network allow it to extract hierarchical features. Our visual system is organized hierarchically. Our brain picks up simple blobs and edges before it picks up shapes (such as squares and circles) and then moves on to facial features or other more advanced concepts. Deep neural networks essentially mimic this functionality. If we take a look at the kind of processing that the middle layers of deep neural network are doing, then we can see that they extract a hierarchy of features. This is why deep neural networks have been so successful in computer vision and language applications. These are domains where by nature are dominated by hierarchical features. ConvNet Playground25 has a model explorer that allows you to see how the different layers of Inception (a famous deep neural network) create more and more complicated representations of an image as the network gets deeper.

However, deep neural networks are not a cure-all.26 If the domain is not characterized by multiple interacting variables, or by hierarchies of features, or there is not enough data, then deep neural networks are probably an overkill. So, if, for example, you have a dataset of 1000 rows and 10 variables, you are much better off using a simpler model (e.g., linear regression), since this model will train faster, and it is less likely to overfit.

Overfitting27 is the bane of all machine learning algorithms and refers to a situation where the performance in the real world is much worse than during training. More complicated models can suffer from this problem. This is why deep neural networks require excessive tuning and testing to make sure they work well.

Statistics

The other core field of data science, statistics, is a branch of mathematics that started around the 18th century and was the first attempt to systematically analyze data. It produced the cornerstones of all modern data analysis, including summary statistics, regression and classification, significant testing, forecasting, and more.

What Makes Statistics Unique?

Statistics generally deal with smaller samples, in large part due to historical reasons. The Internet makes it possible to collect a lot of data nowadays, but in the "olden" days, data usually had to be collected in person, which is why sample sizes were so small.

The results were then extrapolated to the entire population with a margin of error. Also, consider that it was developed in the 17th century, which meant everything had to be calculated by hand.28 Solving a model would take days or weeks.

Statistics is also very strict on model assumptions and development, because it is rooted in math. It's almost like classic AI in this sense. This gap did narrow after parts of machine learning were founded on Bayesian statistics.

However, the mentality still differs. In machine learning, it's all about getting it done and asking questions later. In statistics, though, assumptions must be validated and verified before anything else can be done.

While statistics offers a higher degree of transparency and interpretability, machine learning has led to incredible performance. This amazing performance has allowed us to perform tasks previously thought impossible!

Of course, one has to remember that machine learning is the product of the computer era, which means much faster calculations. Instead of it taking days of work for a single model, it takes minutes—if that—and multiple approaches can be tried in a single day.

The Battle: Statistics vs. Machine Learning

Some statisticians are incredibly opposed to machine learning.29 Religiously opposed. Sometimes, it's actually a bit worrisome. Their problem is the lack of transparency in machine learning as well as a lack of theory.

However, in reality, statistics and machine learning are two sides of the same coin. Furthermore, they are tools in a data scientist's toolbox and can be applied as the situation requires. So, if you are looking for interpretability, then statistics is your best bet, while predictive power will be better served by machine learning.

Subfields of Data Science

In parallel to the development of the aforementioned core fields of data science, other fields were also being developed. These were all related in some way to data analysis, artificial intelligence, and so on. Such fields include cybernetics developed by Norbert Wiener in 1947, artificial neural networks thanks to McCulloch and Pitts in 1943, computational intelligence developed in 1990, machine learning developed in 1959, and data mining and knowledge discovery in databases thanks to Gregory Piatetsky-Shapiro in 1990.30

The problem with all these terms is that not everyone perceives them in the same way necessarily or the relationship between them. In some cases, there are conceptual differences between them, but sometimes it's a matter of who the person talking about them is and what their research background is. There's also the matter of marketing, which can also give a different spin to a particular subfield.

For example, some people consider AI as the core field with natural language processing, expert systems, neural networks, fuzzy logic, and robotics as satellite fields. Others consider that AI is part of computer science, while curated knowledge, machine learning, and reverse engineering the brain are essential to AI. Yet others believe machine learning, deep learning, and representation learning to be contained within AI.

In other words, people have different interpretations of what all these technical terms mean and how they relate to each other, which can make it very confusing. To further prove my point, the following is a definition for computational intelligence at the 11th UK Workshop on Computational Intelligence:

Computational Intelligence (CI) is an offshoot of artificial intelligence in which the emphasis is placed on heuristic algorithms such as fuzzy systems, neural networks and evolutionary computation. It is usually contrasted with 'traditional', 'symbolic' or 'good old fashioned artificial intelligence (GOFAI)'. The IEEE Computational Intelligence Society uses the tag-line 'Mimicking Nature for Problem Solving' to describe Computational Intelligence, although mimicking nature is not a necessary element. In addition to the three main pillars of CI (fuzzy systems, neural networks and evolutionary computation), Computational Intelligence also encompasses elements of learning, adaptation, heuristic and meta-heuristic optimization, as well as any hybrid methods which use a combination of one or more of these techniques. More recently, emerging areas such as artificial immune systems, swarm intelligence,

chaotic systems, and others, have
been added to the range of Computational Intelligence techniques. The term 'Soft Computing' is sometimes used almost interchangeably with
Computational Intelligence.[31]

Now, let's take a look at the definition for Knowledge Discovery in Databases:

The term Knowledge Discovery in Databases, or KDD for short, refers to the broad process of finding knowledge in data, and emphasizes the "high-level" application of particular data mining methods. It is of interest to researchers in machine learning, pattern recognition, databases, statistics, artificial intelligence, knowledge acquisition for expert systems, and data visualization. The unifying goal of the KDD process is to extract knowledge from data in the context of large databases.[32]

The bolded terms show the overlap between all the fields and subfields to the point where some of the core fields are considered subfields of the subfields. Yes, it's confusing and that's exactly the point.

All these fields are interdisciplinary in the sense that they borrow tools from each other, and though they might sometimes take a different approach, there is still so much overlap that it is incredibly problematic. It's even confusing for the people who study these fields.

Take Pattern Recognition and Machine Learning by Christopher M. Bishop,33 which was one of the most important textbooks for machine learning. Everyone has read it, and yet, one has to wonder at the difference between pattern recognition and machine learning. However, once you get into it, you realize that it gets into statistical theory and, generally, just makes things much more complicated. And that's not even close to the end of the matter. There are many other related popular buzzwords and fields, such as

· Natural language processing, which is a subfield of machine learning focused solely on language —generally it relies on text but can also include speech.
· Recommender systems, which is a field dedicated to the study of recommendation engines like the ones used by Amazon and Netflix.
· Predictive analytics, which isn't a sub-discipline but a term that refers mainly to the development of predictive models, that is, algorithms that can predict the future. The latter can be developed using either machine learning or statistics. In other words, it's all really, really confusing, which is where the term "data
science" comes in.

Data Science: The Skills Needed

Data science makes it much easier to explain everything, unless one wants to spend half an hour explaining all the fields and subfields. Even then, most people aren't going to understand, especially if they're not in related fields.
It's much simpler to say one is a data scientist who does stuff with data. It's certainly a lot better than going into a lengthy litany about knowing machine learning, data mining, statistics, and so on. However, even data science is not an infallible term and can cause a little confusion. Some might think that data engineering, databases, big data, and data analysts are pretty much the same thing. But they aren't. So, what are the differences? Well, let's take a look at what these terms mean.

• Data Scientist

A data scientist is someone who works with data. However, this term has been expanded lately to refer to someone who analyzes data but who also has some form of advanced training in a related field, such as a PhD in machine learning or a master's in statistics.

• Data Engineer

A data engineer is someone who designs, builds, and manages the infrastructure for the information of big data. This is the person who develops the architecture that helps analyze and process data. To make a cooking analogy, the data scientist is the chef, while the data engineer encompasses all the tool manufacturers (knives, pots, pans, stoves, etc.) and ingredient vendors who provide the chef with everything he or she needs to create a dish.

• **Big Data**

Big data is a buzzword as it simply refers to massive datasets that are so large and complicated; traditional data processing application software simply can't handle them. It relates to NoSQL databases, cloud computing, Hadoop, and so on.

Table 2-1 shows the important skills for the different categories of data professionals.

Table 2-1. Important skills for different categories of data professionals, ranked out of 3.

	Data analyst	Machine learning engineer	Data engineer	Data scientist
Programming tools	1/3	3/3	3/3	3/3
Data intuition	3/3	3/3	1/3	3/3
Data visualization	3/3	2/3	1/3	3/3
Statistics	2/3	2/3	0/3	3/3
Machine learning	0/3	3/3	0/3	3/3
Software engineering	0/3	2/3	3/3	2/3
Data wrangling	0/3	3/3	3/3	3/3
Mathematics	0/3	3/3	0/3	2/3
Databases	0/3	1/3	3/3	2/3

What Does a Data Scientist Need to Know?

We will delve much more into data scientists later on in this book, but here is a quick overview. While data scientists can come from varied backgrounds, you will usually find three types.
First you have the statisticians, some of which don't like to be called data scientists.
Then you have people with computer science backgrounds who studied machine learning and have either master's degrees or PhDs in the field.
Lastly, you have people coming from other disciplines, like physics; you learned to use data science tools and migrated into the field.

THE QUESTION OF GENERAL ARTIFICIAL INTELLIGENCE

One of the hottest trending topics of our time is "general artificial intelligence." This term refers to the creation of artificial intelligence that can be just as smart as we are. People who believe that this is achievable in the foreseeable future also believe in the concept of a "singularity." A singularity in physics is defined as a moment when the physical models break down (e.g., a situation that exists in the center of a black hole). A technological singularity is a situation where everything we know about society and technology will break down, and something new and unpredictable will show up.
This is based on the following kind of reasoning. While we, humans, possess intelligence, we are limited in our cognitive capacity. We can't hold an infinite size of information in our brain. We can think fast, but not faster than a computer makes calculations. Also, we can get tired, and we need

to sleep.

A general artificial intelligence will have our own ability to think, but none of our limitations. Hence, if a machine had the intelligence of a gifted mathematician, then, in theory, it could come up with a huge number of mathematical theorems within seconds. It could develop capabilities and make inventions that would take humans many lifetimes to achieve. There are people, like Elon Musk or the late Stephen Hawking, who have described AI as a threat to humanity. On the other hand, other people are more optimistic about the potential of general AI to change life for the better.

Irrespective of which side is true, there are a few things that all experts agree on now:

1. We don't have a clear path to general AI. There is not a single method or technology that is guaranteed to achieve this result.
2. Based on the current technological progress, it is very likely that we will see general AI being achieved within our century.
3. While the results of general AI might not be as dramatic as some people expect, everyone agrees that there will be huge disruption in multiple areas: from health research to military.

We are definitely living in interesting times!

Data Management

CHAPTER 3

Data Management

Data management includes all the disciplines involved in working with data and treating it as the valuable resource that it is. A more formal definition is provided by DAMA International,1 which is the professional organization for the profession of data management. Thus, their definition is as follows:

Data Resource Management is the development and execution of architectures, policies, practices and procedures that properly manage the full data lifecycle needs of an enterprise.

So, to talk of data management, we must start with the beginning, and that is understanding where data comes from.

Understanding Where Data Comes From

As previously mentioned, we generate a lot of data. Pretty much everything you do generates some form of data. Companies, for example, collect data from internal sources such as transactions, log data, and emails, but also from external sources such as social media, audio sources, as well as photos and videos.

Other sources of data include

- Published data from credible sources such as government agencies, firms, and industrial associations
- Designed experiments conducted in controlled environments.
- Surveys
- Observations
- Automatic, such as user interactions with applications
- Manual entry, which is effectively people inputting information into the system

These sources of data can be further classified by collection methods.

Data Collection Methods

There are two main types of data collection, namely, observational and experimental.

Observational data collection means that data is gathered passively with no attempt to control the variables involved. For example, collecting customer feedback for a book and a retailer analyzing customer behavior are observational collection methods as there is no attempt to control any variable. Infact, the majority of the data collected by companies is done via observational
methods.

Experimental data collection involves designing and conducting an experiment where certain variables are controlled while you study other variables. This is most common in academic circles but also in clinical settings. A perfect example of it is when a pharmaceutical company tests a new drug. They set up experiments where they control certain variables, like the people involved in the study, and they test other variables, such as the effectiveness of the drug and potential side effects.

In business, experimental data gathering is less prevalent.
A/B testing is one example of this type of data collection where two variables are tested against each other. For example, a company might test the headline of an article against a different headline to see which is more effective at drawing in traffic.

Data Acquisition Considerations

When it comes to data acquisition, there are certain considerations that you need to take into account. Each one is essential and, as you will see later, they can go so far as to affect your whole business model. These are

1. Appropriateness of the data
2. Nature of the data
3. Time requirement
4. Cost of acquisition

So, let's take a look at each of these and what they mean.

Appropriateness of the Data

If you study machine learning, one of the first sayings you will learn is "garbage in, garbage out." In other words, no matter how amazing your algorithm is, if you don't have the right data, then you aren't going to get the right results. So, let's say you're a retailer, and you want to determine the average transaction size per customer for a particular store, which means you need to analyze the transactions for that store. If you enter the data for the wrong store or input customer feedback instead, then you aren't going to get the results you are looking for. This is a bit of a simplistic and extreme example, but the point is that if you put garbage into your model, the algorithm can't turn it into gol, and you will get garbage out the other end.
Now, it might not seem like a big deal, but this happens more often than you realize in the sense that problems are often difficult or impossible to solve because the right data isn't available. This is why it's so essential to keep this point in mind.

Nature of the Data

In some fields, data collection is inherently noisy or biased. For example, consumer surveys and election polling usually deliver biased results. This can be caused by the respondents, but also by the design of the survey, leading to noisy data that's biased from both sides.
Even in more rigid fields, like robotics, there can still be noise when it comes to the measurements made. Of course, this bias and noise can impact the results, which is why it's important to be aware of them. If you don't realize they exist, you won't correct them and the results will be skewed.

Time Requirement

Time requirement refers to how long it takes to collect the data. This is more important in some fields than others, as data collection can be time-consuming. The problem is that in certain situations, it can take so long to collect the data that once you do get it, it might not be useful anymore.

Cost of Acquisition

The cost of acquisition is also an essential component, and it also ties in with the time requirement. The faster you want to get your hands on the data, the more it will cost you. While in some situations the added cost is worth it, in some cases it simply doesn't make sense to pay a lot more to speed up data collection. In some situations, no matter how much you pay, there's no way to make data collection faster.

CASE STUDY: DATA ACQUISITIONPROBLEMS

The aforementioned points don't exist in isolation and often interact with each other. The problem is that if you don't take them all into account, you could end up with a business model that doesn't work.

For example, let's say that you've got a brilliant idea for a startup. You want to make money from sports betting by predicting football outcomes in real time

while the game is being played.
So, you want to develop machine learning models to analyze data in real time to determine who will win, how many corners will be won in the second half, and so on. Then, you can bet accordingly and hopefully make a ton of cash. To achieve this, though, you need data so you check around with vendors to see what predefined packages they offer. For each one, you need to consider the aforementioned points.

Thus, you start with appropriateness of the data. You have to make sure that the data you are getting from your vendor includes the variables you need to make the appropriate predictions. The second point is the nature of the data. In sports, data mistakes are very common, especially if you want real-time data. The more mistakes you plug into your predictive model, the bigger the chances will be that the forecasted outcomes are wrong.

Third is the factor of time requirement. It could take, for example, 10 minutes to get the data after something happened. So, you can't actually get the data in real time or even within a few minutes. Ten minutes might not sound like much, but if you are trying to predict the various outcomes of a game while it is being played, a 10-minute delay could seriously impact the timeliness of your results. After all, getting your prediction after the game is concluded will not help you in any way.

And last but not least is the issue of cost of acquisition. To get data faster, you can pay more, but you have to consider whether the additional cost is worth it or not. This is even more important when you consider that the difference in costs can be as much as five times between post-game data and real-time data.

Furthermore, real-time data also has an increased chance of introducing errors, which can further magnify the cost of the data by generating skewed results.
When you take the above into account, you have to consider what your next step will be. For example, it might be a better idea to purchase data post game instead of trying to predict outcomes in real time.

Not only is this more cost-effective
in terms of the actual cost of buying the data, but it also reduces the chances of skewed results. Post-game data is always more accurate because it is double and triple-checked to ensure accuracy. However, if you do take this route, then you have to consider whether it's still worth getting into this business because there are so many other companies doing the same thing.

And you arrived at this conclusion because you took into account data acquisition considerations, which have shown you that there's a good chance you won't be successful with your idea of real-time sports betting predictions. The advantage is, of course, that you discover these issues before you actually lose money on a model that won't work in the current climate.

Quantitative vs. Qualitative Research

Another important distinction in data acquisition is quantitative and qualitative research. However, these two areas aren't just about how the data is collected but also the type of data and how it is analyzed.

Quantitative Research

Quantitative research is all about numbers. As the name implies, it involves quantifying everything. If you want to know how many people liked a movie, for example, then you turn to quantitative research. If you want to discover how many people buy their groceries online and the frequency with which they do it, then you use quantitative research.

So, quantitative research is used to quantify attitudes, opinions, behaviors, and other defined variables. The advantage is that because of the structured nature of the methods used to collect the data, a larger sample population can be used.

These methods include things like

- Surveys (online, paper, mobile, kiosk surveys)
- Using pre-existing databases (census data)
- Online polls
- Automatic data collection in apps

Quantitative research is great for testing assumptions and getting numbers. However, it's not as good at discovering new insights. Even when you use open-ended questions in quantitative research, you still can't delve deeper like you can with qualitative research. Let's say you've designed a new ad and you want to see what people think of it. You might ask an open-ended question like

If you don't like the ad, what is that you don't like specifically?
You'll get lots of different answers from people, but that's pretty much how far you can go. Someone might say they don't like the colors as a simple example. Because of the nature of quantitative research, you have to move on to the next question and can't dig deeper to find out what they dislike about the colors. Sometimes, the insights you can glean from digging really deep can be very enlightening and not always what you thought they would be.

Qualitative Research
Qualitative research doesn't involve numbers or numerical data and is much more free-form. It's all about words and language, but also pictures and photographs. This is the type of research you turn to when you want to understand people's underlying motivations, reasons, and opinions.

Data collection methods tend to be unstructured or semi-structured such as:

- Individual interviews or group discussions
- Participation/observation
- Pictures, photographs, videos, and so on

With qualitative research, the sample size tends to be smaller and respondents are selected to fulfill a given quota. Traditionally, it wasn't convenient to go with a larger sample size though things are changing thanks to the Internet.
Before, the most common approach to gathering qualitative data was through interviews and group discussions with a trained interviewer. So, to even be able to come close to the sample size of a quantitative project, you'd need a lot of qualified and experienced personnel, as well as a lot of time, making it unfeasible.
Nowadays, though, there are many other options to gather qualitative data because of the Internet. Thus, this data can be gathered via social media and pretty much through everything

your target market posts online, making it easier to use a larger sample size.

DEBUNKING THE MYTH THAT QUANTITATIVE DATA IS BETTER THAN QUALITATIVE DATA

A common assumption is that quantitative research is better than qualitative research because it is quantifiable and can use larger sample sizes. Some also believe this because they think that the structured nature of the collection methods makes the data easier to analyze and less biased.

Nothing could be further from the truth.
First of all, as we've already discussed, sample sizes are no longer as limited as they used to be. Secondly, qualitative data can also be analyzed quite easily nowadays thanks to natural language processing for text data and computer vision for images and video.

For example, you can use deep neural networks to extract emotions from thousands of images and videos or use topic modeling to find the most common process of conversation in a corpus of text (e.g., articles mined from the Web). This process is no longer as subjective as it used to be in the past (when a human had to do all the work), since it is done through machine learning algorithms.

Also, it's very important to note that quantitative data can be still be biased or noisy. Questionnaires with Likert scales or ones that include leading questions, for example, can lead to a glut of quantitative data that is completely biased. Sometimes, respondents to questions deliberately lie. Measurements from devices can be noisy.

Therefore, the lesson is: don't always trust quantitative data, and don't always consider qualitative data to be worthless!

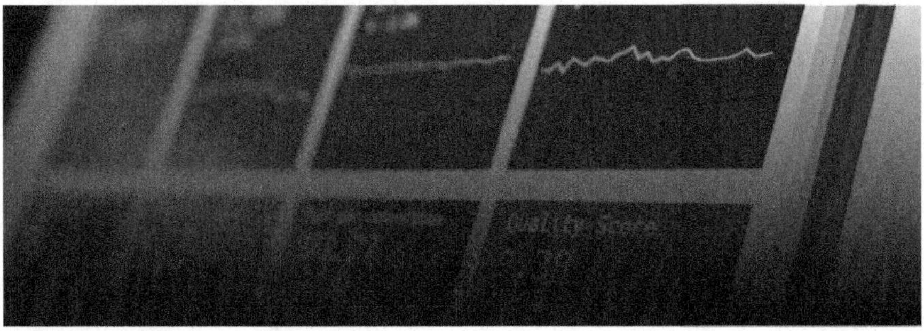

Data Collection Problems

CHAPTER 4

Data Collection Problems

Like with any task, data collection comes with its share of problems that can lead to issues further down the line. While the following list of issues is by no means exhaustive, it does encompass the most common problems that arise in data collection.

First of all, there's the issue of data not being recorded properly. This could be owed to anything from human error when inputting data to noisy sensors, depending on the field. This, of course, causes problems because of the garbage in–garbage out principle.

Another issue is that the data collection isn't supervised by the appropriate principal investigator. When no one who knows the ultimate objective of the project is there to check how and what data is being collected, it can lead to noise and mistakes. If there is monitoring and verification, the potential for mistakes is reduced significantly.

Data isn't always documented, meaning that there are no clear explanations for what each field represents. This makes it difficult for new entrants into the project to understand what's going on and to get up to speed quickly. The delays then slow the whole project down and can even lead to skewed results if the new entrants make the wrong assumptions.

Then there are the legal requirements involved. In many cases, data isn't held in a way that is compliant with the law, such as GDPR that is huge in the United Kingdom and in Europe. This could potentially cause huge problems later down the line.

Another common problem is when the data is kept only by a specific person rather than being in a centralized system. For example, let's say that the project leader is the only one with the data but his laptop is stolen. The result is all that data is lost, which wouldn't have been an issue if it was stored in a centralized system.

Finally, we get to data being stored in multiple places from different sources, which makes consolidation virtually impossible. This is why an integrated system is so important because it makes consolidation much easier and much cheaper.

Data Collection Examples
Now, let's take a look at some data collection examples. We're going to look at six different areas and how data is collected in each, and we'll also look at the advantages and disadvantages of each approach.

B2C Apps
So, let's start with B2C apps, namely, apps created by businesses for the general consumer. The data collected from these apps is usually from registered users and also from how these users

interact with the app.

With data collection via B2C apps, the main advantage is that the data is accurate because no humans are involved, which eliminates the potential for human error.

Of course, there is an exception and that is when users have to register. When users enter their information, there is the potential not just for error but also for users lying. Some users simply don't want to tell you too much about themselves and they have been known to make up things, which can skew your results.

Now, the disadvantage is that the data is only semi-structured, like JSON and XML. The problem is that while the data might follow a pattern, it's not very strictly structured, like having it in a table format. This creates an issue for data scientists because it's not always easy to figure out how to manipulate the data or even what variables should be collected.

For example, a data scientist would have to figure out if every button press and swipe is relevant and should be collected. This is important because the more data you collect, the longer it takes to wrangle it into something that can be analyzed and converted into valuable insights. It can take days or even weeks to get the data under control and translate it into something useful.

Sales

In sales, data is often collected using a CRM, that is, a customer relationship management tool. While some companies might have a different type of tool—or they at least call it something different—in essence, it's still the same thing. In other words, it's a system where customer data is recorded. There's also company data obtained from various databases or other sources, such as UK Companies House or databases like Orbis. The advantage to sales data is that it is generally easy to interpret. You have things like number of units sold, number of calls, average transaction value, and so on. It's pretty straightforward.

However, the problem is that it isn't always clear how the data can be used to provide answers to questions. For example, in your CRM you might have notes on each client, and it might not always be clear how to turn those notes into something useful. It's not impossible by any stretch of the imagination, but it isn't always as straightforward as it might seem.

Retail

Then we move on to retail, where you have sales data—essentially data collected from transactions—as well as customer data.

The main advantage is, like with the aforementioned sales data, the data is pretty straightforward and easy to interpret. You have number of units sold, transaction values, and so on.

However, there are legal considerations to take into account with retail data. For a retailer, the more data they have, the better. But it can be difficult to identify it down to the individual. And this can be, in large part, due to legal frameworks that limit the way retailers can use the data they collect.

Finance

In finance, there's stock market data. This is probably the best area for data collection because the process is automated, the data is clean, and it comes fast. It's one of the few areas where it's virtually impossible to find problems with data collection.

Sports

Then there's data collected in sports, which can be player data that is obtained using an external provider, such as OPTA or STATS.

While sports data is structured and relatively easy to interpret, the main problem is that it is entered manually. In other words, people sit and watch the game and then record the data. This, of course, can result in mistakes and often does as humans are prone to error.

Social Media

Last but not least, we have social media. As you can imagine, this is data sourced from platforms like Facebook, Twitter, Instagram, Pinterest, and so on. The advantage to social media is that data collection is automated. All you have to do, basically, is plug in an API and off you go. However, the problem arises when you try to make sense of all the data you collected. It's completely unstructured and really, really noisy and messy.

If you've ever worked with any form of social media data, like Facebook posts, tweets, and even blog comments, you've likely seen a wide range of issues. You have grammar issues, different languages, special characters and emoticons, and so on. As you can imagine, this can make it very difficult to wrangle the data into something useful and easily analyzed. It definitely takes a lot of time to do so.

Data Management Practices

Now, let's take a closer look at data management. There are both good and bad practices in data collection and storage, and we'll be looking at some of these.

However, it's important to note that we aren't going to be looking at good and bad practices from a technical standpoint as this isn't a book about data engineering. We'll be analyzing these practices from a business viewpoint, and once we're done, we'll also take a look at some examples of bad practices and good practices.

Good Practices for Data Collection and Organization

Good practices in data collection and organization mainly revolve around having an objective before you start, being aware of how data collection affects the rest of your business, and creating a standard. Let's examine each one of these elements.

Establish a Goal First

When it comes to data collection and organization from a business perspective, it is essential to first establish at least one goal or have one question to answer. Otherwise, you will end up collecting data that you might not need or the wrong data.

So, before you do anything, you need to establish an objective. Before you ask, "let's collect some data because that's what everyone seems to be doing" is not an objective. On the other hand, "why do 35% of our customers not go through with the purchases in their cart?" is a good objective/ question to start with.

Awareness of How Data Collection Affects the Rest of Your Business

It's also essential to be aware of how data collection interacts with other parts of the business, such as the user interface. We'll be talking more about this later.

Establish a Data Standard

You also want to use a data standard and document everything that is happening. By creating a data standard everyone can easily understand, new project entrants can quickly get up to speed, saving you significant amounts of time and resources in the long run.

Bad Practices for Data Collection and Organization

Bad practices are pretty much the exact opposite of the good practices I described earlier. Let's take a closer look at each.

No Clear Objective

Having no clear objective from the start means you just collect data for the sake of it with no clear direction and take the "we'll store the data now and think about it later" approach. This is pretty much a waste of time and resources.

Ignoring the Connection Between Data Collection and the Rest of Your Business

The next issue is not taking into account the connection between data and business. You might think that the data won't affect the business at all, but this is completely erroneous. For example, if you want to build a better recommender system and to collect data to this end, you might have to completely rebuild the UI. Nothing in your business exists in a vacuum, including and especially data collection.

No Documentation or Data Standard

Finally, the most common bad practice is having no documentation or data standard in place, which makes it difficult for anyone new to the project to understand what's going on.

Examples of Bad Practices or What You Shouldn't Do!

In this first example, we'll take a look at how lacking a clear objective can derail your efforts and cost you money.

Lack of Clear Objective

Let's take a B2C app that helps users find restaurants in their country or city as an example. You run and manage this app and you decide to collect data from users. You have no idea what you're going to use the data for, but you figure that it will be useful at some point in the future.

You decide to register the information in a NoSQL database in JSON format. You collect their name and age, like {"name": John, "age": 23}. However, you decide to collect the data.

Thus, you now have their name and age, and you also have their app interactions, like when they open the app, scroll through it, make a selection, and so on.

One day, a year after you launched the B2C app, you decide you should find a data scientist to help you with the data. So, you hand over the data you've collected to the data scientist and ask them to extract general insights.

You might be wondering what's wrong with this approach—it doesn't seem to be problematic, does it? Well, there are actually quite a few issues.

This is one of the most frustrating situations to be in when someone is a data scientist. Why is that? Well, first off, you haven't optimized the data to achieve any particular goal, which means that data scientists will waste a lot of time trying to figure out what they can do with the data and how they can do it.

The data wrangling will also take a really, really long time. And this will be time that costs you money, whether you are outsourcing to an independent data scientist or have hired a full-time person for the position.

Finally, you opted to use NoSQL as the format for data storage, and this might not necessarily be the best option depending on what you want to do with the data. So, this will make it even harder for the data scientist to wrangle the data and it will certainly take a lot longer.

But I Have an Objective!

Okay, so let's take the same B2C app from the previous example and assume you have an objective. That should make it easier to wrangle all that data into something useful, right? Well, not really.

Let's say that your goal is to build a recommender system so you hand the data over to the data scientist who should be pleased that you have a
specific goal you want to achieve. What's wrong now?

While it's certainly a little better than the previous example because you do have an objective you want to achieve, issues will still arise. First of all, the data might not be in a format that is optimized to develop a recommender system. This means that the data scientist will have to try to wrangle the data into submission to get it in a format that is usable.

Furthermore, if you collected data willy-nilly without knowing the objective in advance, you might not even have the right variables available. You have age, name, and interactions, but what about gender? Does gender even matter in recommending a restaurant? Of course it does.

Here's a really extreme example. Say, you have a number of "restaurants" registered that provide adult entertainment for women, a.k.a. male strippers. . How happy would you be if you were searching for a family-friendly restaurant and saw a strip club "restaurant" in the list of recommendations? Not exactly overly pleased, right?

And yes, we know that a lot of other variables would be important in the previous example, but it just goes to further prove the point that you need to collect a lot more data to create an effective recommender system.

Another variable you'd definitely need is location. What's the point of recommending a restaurant in New York to someone who lives in Austin? A recommendation like that isn't of much use, and it will also alienate your users because they'll quickly realize your recommender system is a complete waste of time.

Yes, a number of these variables can be inferred, but it is very time-consuming and prone to errors. So, it would have been a much better option to collect this information from the start.
The conclusion is that a little advanced planning can save you lots of pain in the long run. Remember, as with everything, failing to plan is planning to fail when it comes to data collection.

CASE STUDY: BAD PRACTICES IN DATA MANAGEMENT
Some of the things discussed in this chapter might seem too obvious. However, the kind of problem you can encounter in your daily professional life might surprise you. Here's an example from personal experience—just in case you think stuff like this doesn't happen in the real world.

A few years ago, a client wanted me to study the difference between male and female behavior on their platform. Do males take more actions X than females?
Or do females consume more than males on the platform?

This is a relatively straightforward problem which can be answered through simple statistical means such as hypothesis tests. However, things were not as simple as it would have been expected.

Gender wasn't a variable that was collected and stored in the database. So, the objective of the study was to understand the differences between genders, but this variable was non-existent!

The solution that was devised was to infer gender from the names of the users. However, in a multicultural place such as London (where this company was based), this is much harder than it sounds. There are so many nationalities living in London, which makes it impossible to cover all the names by using a simple name registry.

Unfortunately, even after using name registries from multiple countries (ranging from the United Kingdom, to the United States, to Nigeria, to India, and more) we still had to throw away 30% of the data. The reason was that some names could not be found in the registries and that some names are used by both males and females.

Therefore, what should have been a straightforward piece of research suddenly turned into something very complicated. And the root of all these causes was the lack of planning and the lack of a data strategy. Failing to plan is planning to fail.

So, whatever you do, do not be like this client. Plan your needs in advance so you don't waste your time and resources or end up with unusable data and skewed results.

Examples of Good Practice or What You Should Do!
This is the perfect time to discuss what you should do. Coming back to our restaurant B2C app, it would have made life easier for everyone if the data strategy had been established from the beginning.

Data Collection Problems

So, whatever app or business you run, you need to think in advance of what you might need. With the restaurant B2C app, it would have been clear from the start that a recommender system would be necessary at some point. And the same holds true for most of these apps.

If you have no idea what you might need in the future, you can just hire a data scientist to consult. It might cost you a few hours of consultation, but it's going to save you a significant amount of pain down the line. It'll also definitely be cheaper because setting everything up right from the start will always be cheaper than fixing the problems in the future.

Another issue is with the technology being used. Why choose NoSQL if for certain things SQL is much easier to deploy and use, like for user registration data? It's like using a grenade to kill a fly instead of a fly swatter or fly spray. It might get the job done but it's definitely overkill and will create a much bigger mess.

Finally, you need to be aware of all the variables you might need in the future. Storage is cheap and it's better to have more information than you need rather than omitting data and not recording variables that might be critical to future projects.

Obviously, you can't think of everything in advance, but it's still a good exercise to try to do as much as possible.

Don't Buy the Hype!

This is a very important point. In computer science, new technology is being developed constantly, and something new and shiny pops up every few years. For example, for big data, we saw the development of NoSQL databases, while machine learning gave us deep learning.

While these technologies are extremely powerful, they've been created to deal with specific issues. The problem is that there are companies out there that want you to buy their brand new shiny products and services and will say just about anything to convince you that you need them, even when you don't need tech that advanced.

This is quite a common issue. There are so many companies out there using NoSQL solutions, for example, when they don't really need it. Of course, this doesn't mean you should never use these technologies. It just means that you should think about it twice and make sure you really do need them.

For example, NoSQL generally assumes that you want to store big amounts of data and it's difficult to express the structure in a table format. So, if you don't have ridiculous amounts of data, it might not make sense to go with NoSQL. Also, choosing the right NoSQL database is not an easy task. Just by searching the Internet, you can find more than ten different options, with more coming. There are some cases where using a NoSQL solution makes perfect sense (e.g., graph data or when you are storing posts from social media), but don't just do it without thinking. In most cases you are just fine with some simple implementation of SQL, such as MySQL.8.

Deep learning is another example. It's great technology but should only be applied in certain situations, like for images, audio, and video. Otherwise, it requires a lot of computational resources, which means it can get expensive and time-consuming to develop a deep neural network.

In other words, don't use technology just because it's new and shiny and a slick sales rep has spent an inordinate amount of time convincing you that you absolutely need it. Instead, take a step back and take an objective look at if you really need that type of tech.

If you don't, it's better to go with a trusted solution that has been available for a longer period of time because it's been thoroughly tested and proven to work effectively. Plus, it will also be easier to hire people to work with said technology because there are more people who have expertise working with it.

Setting Goals in Advance

Failing to plan is planning to fail. This is one of my favorite phrases when it comes to data strategy.

If I haven't yet made my point, I'll say it again: it's essential to think about what you might want to do with the data in the future.

It's definitely not easy to think in advance of all the types of data you might need to solve a problem, and it can take time. However, it more than pays off to sit down and think about it.

For example, you might need 20 variables to create an outstanding recommender system for your app. If you didn't take time to think about it, you might have 3 of these variables. Conversely, if you did sit down and plan in advance, you might have 15 variables. It's not the full 20 because no one can predict everything in advance, but it's still much better than only 3.

If you really have no clue or don't have the time to engage in this exercise, then hire a data scientist to consult before you start collecting data. Taking this approach is also essential because data collection and data science can interact with other parts of your business and business model. It's not going to take more than a couple of days of the data scientist's time (which means you won't have to spend much money), and it is well worth it.

Examples of the Impact of Data Science and Collection on Your Business

In this section, we're going to look at some examples of how data collection and data science can affect your user interface and can even lead to completely different business models.

Data Science and Dating

So, let's say you have a B2C app in the dating space and you need to create a recommender system for your app.

Consider Tinder, a popular dating app, and OkCupid, which is a popular dating website. It's not important if you aren't familiar with these apps, but they are excellent examples.

From a data science or machine learning perspective, the whole problem with dating is ensuring the system makes the right recommendations.

Tinder, for example, takes a pretty simplistic approach. You can swipe left or right on someone's profile, which tells the system whether you like them or not. However, you don't have a lot of data. You can see their picture, first name, and age, and maybe a few other photos, but that's about it.

OkCupid, on the other hand, has taken a much more in-depth approach. They've created a questionnaire that has a lot of questions. And when I say a lot, I really mean a lot of questions. This questionnaire really digs into your preferences, opinions, and personality. They then use the answers from the questionnaire to match people with each other.

If you're a data scientist and you want to create a recommender system for matchmaking, you're probably going to do something similar to what OkCupid has done.

However, you have to consider the fact that OkCupid is much more difficult to use. The site asks you over a hundred questions, and it's going to take you a while to get through them. So, in terms of data science, OkCupid is a data scientist's dream. The data that OkCupid possesses is so detailed that they have even published research on human sexuality and romantic preferences. However, this does not necessarily make for the smoothest user experience.

Conversely, Tinder might never have a great recommender system because they don't collect enough data to develop one, but they do provide a great user experience. That's where their focus has been and it can be seen quite easily because it takes very little time for users to screen a large number of profiles.

One is not necessarily better than the other. They're just different. But what is important is that these two systems clearly show how data science and data collection affect the user interface, the user experience, and even the whole business model.

And it should be noted that both OkCupid and Tinder are wildly successful. So, it's not a matter of which one is right; it's simply a matter of you taking the time to think about how this works in your own business.

Data Science and Entertainment

Another example is of B2C apps in the entertainment space, more specifically concert finding apps. Recommender systems make it easy to demonstrate how all the different elements interact, which is why we are focusing on them.

With a concert finder, you can scroll through the list of local shows. You tap on a specific show; you have a number of options. You can state that you're attending, you can say maybe you're attending, you can get tickets, or you can share on Facebook or Twitter.

From a user perspective, this might not seem like important information. But for a data scientist, it's a wealth of data—it's like hitting the jackpot.

Every action demonstrates a different kind of involvement. Someone who clicks "I'm attending" is definitely more interested and involved than someone who only says "Maybe." And then there is the combination of actions. Someone might state they are attending and then also share the concert on Facebook, which clearly shows that they really, really love that music and/or performer.

So, the important part is that all this data is stored in a database and can be analyzed to garner important and valuable insights. A data scientist will be able to see all these actions and combinations of actions and draw conclusions that will benefit how the recommender system works.

For example, if someone states they will be attending a Beyoncé concert, gets tickets, and shares on both Facebook and Twitter, then they're going to want to know about every possible Beyoncé concert—in some cases even if it's not a local concert.

However, someone else who simply says they might attend and eventually does get tickets but doesn't share might not be as interested. While you will definitely include local Beyoncé concerts in their recommended list, it might not make sense to tell them about concerts outside their area because they aren't such an avid fan.

So, this information could help a data scientist understand how important the different actions are, for example. This can, of course, be used to later improve the recommendations the system provides.

It can also be used to understand how to convert those who said "Maybe" into ticket buyers. A company could send them offers or rewards or use different methods to change their mind.

This shows how certain aspects of a UI might mean very little to the end user but can be a treasure chest of vital information for a data scientist and can have a significant impact on the success of your business.

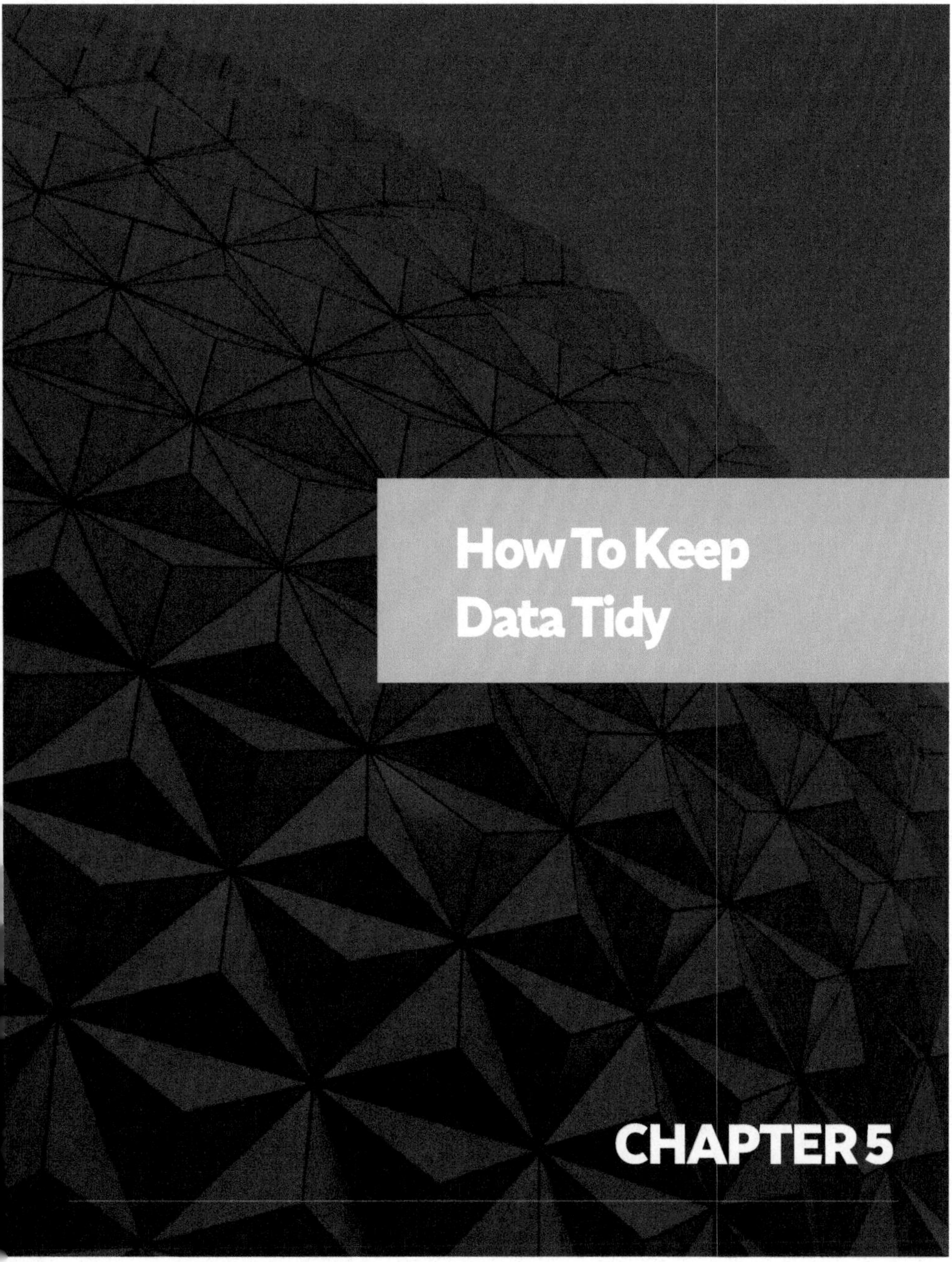

How To Keep Data Tidy

CHAPTER 5

How To Keep Data Tidy

Dirty data refers to data that can suffer from all sorts of problems, including, but not limited to, things such as erroneous or conflicting entries, missing values, and outdated data. Tidy data is the opposite, data that is in a nice format, with no inconsistencies or other issues.

Dirty data can cause all sorts of problems. First, it makes consolidation of different data sources difficult or sometimes outright impossible. Second, many of the data points might not be usable. This can reduce the effective size of your data. You might be holding 5GB of data, but only 1 gigabyte might be usable.

There is another tricky problem that can show up with dirty data. If you create models based on dirty data, then the model will produce results that might not correspond to reality, but you might not be aware that this is happening until it is too late.

For example, you might have deployed a machine learning system in the real world (e.g., a recommender system, or a price optimization tool, or a demand forecasting tool), and it might take you some time before you realize the results do not correspond to reality. However, in the meantime, you have been recommending products (or adjusting prices, or something else) in the wrong way!

This is one of the trickiest parts behind data science models. A wrong model will not fail to compile (like in software development). It will work fine until you realize that the results do not make much sense. This is why planning in advance is so crucial (as we stressed out in the previous section), and keeping your data tidy is part of this plan which you must follow.

In terms of causes, most problems with dirty data are usually caused by

1. Different departments handling the datasets
2. Lack of documentation
3. Lack of communication between different parts of the company

The easiest way to understand dirty data and its potential impact on your organization is to look at a real-world example. This actually did happen like all the examples woven throughout the book.

Let's say you are dealing with data collection and data management in a football club (or soccer club if you're from North America). So, within a football club, you have a medical department, football training, weight training, and the coach.

However, there is no centralized system for collecting or storing the data. All data is collected manually and stored in Excel files, which is very problematic. It's very difficult to format, use, and consolidate the data.

Different people have different files and different datasets. Essentially, the data is all over the place and everyone has bits of it.

There's also a lack of supervision, which means that there is no certainty the variables recorded are accurate.
Then you have limited communication between departments. For example, a player might come back to train after suffering an injury, but might not let the medical department know he's back. So, the medical department believes he's still injured and has him recorded as such in their data.

The departments also have different goals. The medical department wants to protect the player to ensure he is fully healed and won't end up even more hurt if he comes back too soon. Conversely, the coach just wants the player back on the field. So, the medical department could have an incentive to make the injury seem more serious than it actually is, while the coach wants to minimize the importance of the injury.

Lastly, there's no established procedures for data standardization and data entry.

This means there's a certain level of freedom in terms of how the data is being recorded by each department. It can even occur within the same department. Two different doctors, for example, might refer to the same medical issue in two different ways. For a doctor, it might be easy to understand that The Decision Maker's Handbook to Data Science they're talking about the same thing, but for someone who isn't a doctor, it can be a problem. So, a data scientist trying to analyze this data could end up confused.

There's also a lack of transparency. In our case, the medical department had no idea what was happening in the player's schedule. It's not just about the player who didn't inform the medical department he's recovered from his injury. For example, a player could be eating the wrong food, and no one is recording it. Likewise, a player could have been training longer hours without informing them.

Of course, without this vital information, it makes it harder for the medical department to resolve issues and diagnose problems. So, our player with the poor diet could end up having issues with performance, but the medical department can't advise him on a better diet or at least the effects of his current diet on him before it becomes a performance issue because they don't know.

Thus, they ended up with data that was "dirty," which resulted in lots of back-and-forth. A lot of time was spent in meetings between the different departments, trying to sort all the data out before anyone could analyze it properly.

In the meantime, a lot of time was wasted as it took months to clean up and consolidate the data, but worse, a large number of erroneous conclusions were drawn.

Finally, the learning curve was long. First, the mess meant that the overall time of the project to make sense of the data was long. Second, any new people who joined the project took quite a while to get up to speed and to reach a point where they understood what was happening.

Solutions

So, the first solution is to implement a centralized system to store data, but also a single system to collect data. In other words, Excel shouldn't even be a blip on anyone's radar. Furthermore, no more separate files, with each person having their own file on their own computer in their own format.

Now, there's a centralized data storage system, and all data is collected through a single app that everyone uses, with no one recording data manually anymore. This approach has made it easier to enforce a data standard.

Thus, people no longer had that much freedom in how they recorded data. For example, doctors couldn't describe the same medical issue in different ways because they had a limited number of options available in a drop-down list. This minimized the possibility of misunderstandings taking place.

It was also essential to improve communication between the departments. Thus, quick weekly meetings were instituting, essentially "forcing" departments to talk to one another. This helped eliminate issues where a player was actually playing while the medical department still had him recorded as being on leave due to his injury.

So, the solution involved creating a data standard, forcing people to follow the standard, centralize everything, and essentially eliminate silos. When you have silos, it's very easy for misunderstandings to occur, so when you eliminate them, you will find that efficiency increases significantly.

CASE STUDY: MODELS ON DIRTY DATA

This true story can help you understand how dirty data can mess things up. While doing research with a football club, I thought I had discovered a very interesting pattern. Players that were training during the pre-season period seemed to get injured on Mondays after a couple of weeks of training.

I created a statistical model which seemed to validate this conclusion. The working theory was that there must be some kind of shock effect into the body coming back from the off-season and straight into intensive training during the pre-season. Maybe starting training and then being off training for the weekend and coming back to it on Monday increased the likelihood of injury. If that was the case, then the club would have to adjust its training methods or resting protocols for the players. However, my theories were soon confronted with reality. The explanation was much simpler. There was nothing happening with overtraining or other complicated patterns of the athletes being active and inactive which made them more prone to injury.

In many cases injuries would not be detected by the coach or the training staff. Rather, the players had to report the injuries. The team's protocol dictated that if a player reported being injured toward the end of the week, they had to stay in the training facilities for rehabilitation for the whole weekend. However, most players didn't like that. They wanted to just go to a pub or stay at home or whatever it is that they preferred to do with their free time on a weekend. This means that many players that were injured late on Thursday or on Friday would not report the injury on those dates. Rather, they would wait for Monday and they would report they are injured. Hence, the pattern I thought I had discovered had just been caused by the peculiarities of the domain and data collection. Injuries were not objectively measured (rather self-reported). Injuries had been recorded as taking place as soon as they were being reported. For example, if someone was injured on Friday, but reported it on Monday, then the injury was recorded as having taken place on Monday.

A couple of months of work down the drain because of wrong data collection practices and gaps in domain knowledge caused by miscommunication. This is a case where dirty data really messed up the whole plan. Lessons learned? First, when entering a new domain, ask as many questions as possible, as the domain experts will not always remember every relevant detail and explain it to you. Second, make sure you fully understand the data collection and data entry practices. Again, these problems would have been avoided if a proper protocol had been designed from the beginning.

An Introduction To Data Science/AI For The Nontechnical Person

CHAPTER 6

In this chapter we will delve deeper into data science, and discuss what it is, and why it's useful. We will cover the brief history of data science and take a look at the core fields that compose it. The aim of this chapter is to give to the nontechnical reader a good brief overview of that area and understand where it can be applied and why.

Data science is made up of multiple disciplines. So, to get a good grasp of what data science is, we need to look at the core disciplines that make up this field of study. First, though, let's take a quick look at how it all started.

Brief History of Data Science

Though data science became more popular with the increase of data gen-eration, it has been around for a while. Many look to John Tukey as one of the people who pushed the boundaries of statistics and gave birth to the concept of data analysis as a science (Leonhardt 2000).

Tukey wrote The Future of Analysis in 1962, while he was a professor at Princeton University and working at Bell Labs to develop statistical methods for computers (Tukey 1962).

In the article, he encouraged academic statisticians to get involved in the entire process of data analysis instead of just focusing on statisti-cal theory. He pointed out how important it was to distinguish between exploratory and confirmatory data analysis, which was the first step to creating the field of data science.

While others certainly had a significant impact on data science as we know it today, Tukey was among the first to advocate for the importance of such a field. However, it took some time until the early 2000s for data science to really take off. The reason is that the turn of the millennium saw a few trends converging:

1. The rise of the Internet;

2. Cheaper storage and computing power;

3. The rise of cloud computing;

4. The rise in the volumes of data being generated.

The convergence of those four trends made data a valuable resource, with some calling data the new oil. This incentivized the re-emergence of the field of data science as a unifying force into what used to be disparate fields.

The Core Fields of Data Science
Taking a closer look at the history of data science means delving into its three core fields: AI, ML, and statistics. There are many other trends that have risen and fallen over the years: data mining, pattern recognition, cybernetics, and more. These terms often describe scientific approaches that tried to recreate intelligence inside a machine, or developed tech-niques to extract insights from data. However, the primary fields are AI, ML, and statistics, and we will delve into these in more depth over the next few chapters.

A Closer Look at AI
AI is exactly what it sounds like. People are trying to get machines to think like humans. In more technical terms, this means giving a machine the ability to reason logically, self-correct, and learn. Written out as it is, it might sound simple. It isn't. To even come vaguely close to achieving these goals, you need a lot of data and a lot of computing power.

Classic AI came into being in 1956 at Dartmouth College, when five men came together who would go on to become the founders and leaders of AI research. They were Allen Newell (CMU), Herbert Simon (CMU), John McCarthy (MIT), Marvin Minsky (MIT), and Arthur Samuel (IBM) (Russell, Norvig, and Davis 2010; McCorduck 2004).

It really started, though, with Marvin Minsky, who would become known as the father of AI. He wanted to create an intelligent
machine, which we would call AI and define it as the science of mak-ing machines perform tasks that would require intelligence if done by men (Whitby 1996).

To figure out how to achieve such a monumental goal, one must start by understanding the human brain, especially intuition, representing our capacity for logical reasoning.

Logical reasoning refers to the ability to draw logical conclusions based on various facts, such as:

"If all soldiers are in the army, and John is a soldier, then John is in the army."

This is a simple conclusion to draw for a human, of course. However, it's far more complicated for a machine to do it. To do so, humans con-structed a set of rules with which they programmed the computer. Using this rule-based or symbolic approach, reasoning algorithms developed the ability to draw these logical conclusions. This gave birth to the rise of the "expert systems" market.

An early example of an expert system is MYCIN. The system was designed to diagnose infections and figure out what bacteria was the underlying cause.

Developed in the 1970s at Stanford University, the system relied on around 600 rules (Buchanan and Shortliffe 1984). Users would answer a series of questions. Based on these answers, the system would come up with a list of which bacteria could be the culprits. The results would be sorted in order of probability, along with a confidence score and explanations of how the conclusion was reached. The system would also recommend a course of treatment.

At a 69 percent accuracy rate, the system proved to be better at diag-nostics than inexperienced doctors and on par with some experts (Yu, Victor, Fagan, Wraith, Clancey, Scott, Hannigan, Blum, Buchanan, and Cohen 1979).

The system's success relied on the fact that it had been fed a significant amount of data obtained by interviewing clinicians, diagnosticians, and other health care experts, who offered up their experience and expertise. It relied on an IF (condition) THEN (conclusion) methodology.

The system was never used in a clinical setting, though. First, it required a lot of computing power and would still take 30 minutes to come up with a diagnosis. In a real-world environment, this was far too long.
Legal and ethical concerns also came up, mainly connected to who would be liable if the system made a mistake, either in the diagnosis or the recommended treatment.
Despite it not being used in the real world, MYCIN still played an important role because many other rule-based programs in various fields were developed based on it.

Unfortunately, the development of AI experienced a series of setbacks. Otherwise, the field would have been far more advanced. These setbacks are popularly referred to as AI winters and are, basically, periods when the world lost interest in AI.

For example, in 1967, Marvin Minsky was confident that it would take no more than a generation to solve the problem of creating AI. How-ever, by 1982, he was no longer so confident as he admitted it was one of the most difficult problems science had ever faced (Allen 2001).

The two main AI winters that set everything back were between 1974 and 1980 and from 1987 to 1993. The first winter was caused by several events that resulted in the belief that AI didn't have any real-world applications.

The first of these events was a report written by Sir James Lighthill, who believed that AI was a waste of time. He proposed that other sciences could achieve everything AI was doing and went on to imply that even the best algorithms set forth by the field of AI couldn't help with any problems in the real world (Lighthill 1973).

Funding for AI dried up, and, soon after, the 1969 Mansfield Amend-ment was passed in the United States. The amendment stated that DARPA was to only fund research with a clear objective and would result in tech-nological solutions that the military could use. The shorter the timeframe for results, the better.

Using the Lighthill report as further proof that it would be a long while before AI generated anything useful for real-world applications, DARPA stopped funding anything AI-related. In fact, by 1974, it became practically impossible to find even the smallest amount of funding for any AI-based projects (National Research Council (U.S.) 1999).

The Speech Understanding Research program at Carnegie Mellon also contributed to the problem. DARPA's goal had been to obtain a sys-tem that pilots could use to control fighter planes. While the research team came up with a system that understood English, the words had to be said in a particular order. DARPA felt that they had been tricked as the system didn't even come close to what they wanted. So, in 1974, they canceled the grant (Crevier 1993; McCorduck 2004; National Research Council (U.S.) 1999).

By 1985, though, after the commercial success of various expert systems, interest in AI had been rekindled, and more than $1 billion was allocated to AI research. As a result, an entire industry developed to support the field of AI.

Machine Learning: Taking AI to a New Level

While classic AI research led to a wide range of beneficial discoveries and developments, it wasn't really AI as we see in science fiction, with machines that could truly think for themselves. More was required, which is where ML comes in.

Machine learning is what gets us closer to the human brain because it's meant to give a machine the ability to become more than its program-ming. To learn and improve beyond what we've taught it to do.
Therefore, ML is all about developing algorithms that can learn from the information they've been provided with, but that can also draw con-clusions and make predictions pertaining to data they haven't yet analyzed.

Arthur Samuel, a pioneer in AI and computer gaming, first came up with the term of ML in 1959 while working at IBM. He stated that the goal of ML was to provide computers with the ability to learn without being programmed to do so (Samuel 1959).

Machine learning remains a subfield of AI, but the approach it took was virtually the opposite of what had been done so far in AI research.
Classic AI worked with a rule-based, top-down approach, meaning that computers were provided with rules, which they had to follow to get to the desired result. The main concern with this approach was the significant amount of human input necessary.

Essentially, if you're the one designing the system, you have to think of every possible variable and eventuality that could arise and then create a set of rules for it. Unfortunately, since the system uses an IF/THEN approach, it doesn't handle uncertainty well.

This can create significant problems because very few things are quite that straightforward in life, especially if you're trying to create complicated software. IF (EVENT A) occurs, there's no guarantee that THEN (ACTION B) is the best solution or even the solution at all. For example, IF (RAINING) doesn't always lead to THEN (TAKE AN UMBRELLA). After all, you could always stay indoors and avoid the rain altogether.

That's not even the most significant issue. The real problem is that the only reason the system knows to provide this answer is that it has already been told what to do. That isn't in line with the ultimate goal of ML and AI, namely, to create a machine that can think for itself.

In contrast, ML starts at the other end, using a bottom-up, data-driven approach. In other words, in ML, data is used to teach the computer what to do. It's akin to the principle of teaching a man to fish rather than giving him the fish.

With ML, other than feeding the computer the data, there isn't much human input. Therefore, the machine can handle uncertainty more organically, which is the goal because the world consists more of probabilities than certainties.

With our rain/umbrella example, a machine would be fed with tons of data that it would analyze. It would see that, in some cases, when it's raining out, people will take umbrellas. In others, though, they will wait indoors until the rain has passed. It would look for patterns to differenti-ate when each event occurred, and it might discover that with lighter rain and warmer temperatures, people are more likely to brave the weather with an umbrella. However, if it's cold out and raining heavily, people are more likely to stay indoors. It picks up patterns, which it does by learning from the data it has been provided with.

Machine learning became very popular after the widespread adoption of the World Wide Web helped generate unprecedented amounts of data for the first time in human history. This, in combination with cheaper computing costs, has made ML the dominant approach in data science.

These days, AI is practically synonymous with ML

Statistics

Statistics is another core field of data science. It first came about in the 17th 18th centuries and was the first way people analyzed data in an organized, systematic fashion (Willcox 1938). It eventually led to the devel-opment of all the key aspects of modern data analysis, including regression, significant testing, summary statistics, and forecasting.

Traditionally, statistics dealt with small samples, mainly because of when it was developed. It's only relatively recently that we have become able to gather data remotely—at least when you consider how long the field of statistics has been around. When it was first developed, all data collection had to be done in person. Furthermore, everything had to be calculated by hand, so solving a model could take weeks.

The main difference between statistics and ML is that you must first validate and verify your assumptions with statistics. With ML, however, it's all about getting things done and asking questions later. While statistics offers a lot more transparency and interpretability, ML has led to amazing advances and performance.

However, ML does rely on computing, which means that models can be solved in minutes (usually far faster than that) instead of days. There-fore, multiple approaches can be attempted in far shorter time frames, leading to better performance and quicker progress

Other Subfields of Data Science

Besides AI, ML, and statistics, data science also has other subfields, such as:

- Cybernetics, developed by Norbert Wiener in 1947;

- Artificial neural networks developed by McCulloch and Pitts in 1943;

- Computational intelligence developed in 1990;

- Data mining developed by Gregory Piatetsky-Shapiro in 1990 (McCulloch and Pitts 1943; Conway and Siegelman 2005; Russel and Norvig 2003; Samuel 1959; Piatetsky-Shapiro 1994).

The main problem for those not in the field is that all these terms have fluid definitions. Take two people with different research backgrounds, and they'll often give you different definitions for the same thing. While some conceptual differences exist, it often becomes difficult to tell unless you know who's doing the talking. Sometimes, it gets so complicated that even people who study these fields end up confused.

This is where the idea of data science came in. It simply made things a lot easier to explain. Saying a data scientist is someone who works with data is far simpler than trying to explain every field and subfield involved.

The essence of data science is that it allows us to take data and do use-ful things with it. While there are certainly all sorts of complex definitions available that cover tools and methodologies, at its core, data science is all about doing useful things with data.

A Dive Into ML for a Decision Maker

As we've seen, ML is vital to data science and can even be considered the next step up from classic AI. The main objective for ML is to enable computers to learn by being fed data rather than being explicitly programmed to do something.

Machine learning can be split into three major approaches: supervised learning, unsupervised learning, and reinforcement learning (Figure 6.1).

Supervised learning involves showing the machine what you want by providing examples. So, let's say you want it to organize a set of photos by separating them into images with humans and images containing vegetables. You'd provide an example of a photo with a human and one of a vegetable, making sure to label each appropriately. Then, the computer can sort the remaining images based on the labels you provided.

With unsupervised learning, you just provide the computer with the photos and allow it to organize them based on the different traits it can identify itself, without labels or human supervision.

Finally, with reinforcement learning, the system learns by making mistakes and receiving rewards when it gets things right. The computer analyzes the actions it took and the outcomes of those actions.

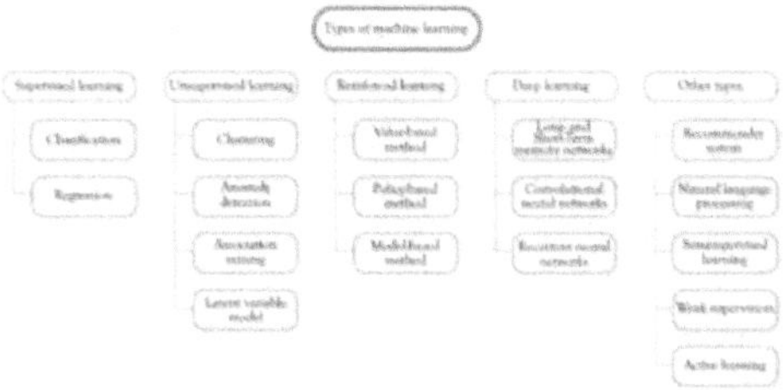

Figure 6.1 Types of machine learning

Supervised Learning

In supervised learning, algorithms learn by example with some form of supervision. It's almost like having a teacher supervising students, except that the students are algorithms in this case.

When you train such an algorithm, you provide training data consist-ing of inputs paired with the correct outputs. The machine will analyze the data in the training phase, looking for patterns that align with the desired outputs. So, you give the computer a bunch of photos of vege-tables, and you tell it what each vegetable is. The computer analyzes this data to determine the pattern that leads to the correct conclusion. It will determine that an eggplant is oblong and dark purple, whereas a tomato is round and red.

Subsequently, after training has been completed, you can feed that algorithm new inputs, and it will classify the new data based on the train-ing data it received. Therefore, it will classify oblong, dark purple objects as eggplants and round, red items as tomatoes.

The role of the supervisor is to correct the algorithm every time it makes a mistake. However, since the algorithm is constantly learning, it will eventually get to the point where it no longer makes mistakes.

It is, by far, the most popular flavor of ML. It is the primary technology used in task automation.

Supervised learning can be split into two categories: classification and regression.

Classification Models

Classification requires the algorithm to be provided with data that has been assigned to categories. The algorithm then takes inputs and assigns the categories based on the provided training data, like our previous example.

In real-world applications, the simplest example would be categorizing emails as spam or not spam, which is a binary classification problem.

The way it works is that the algorithm is provided with e-mails that are spam and emails that are not spam. It looks for the common features among each category. It will then use these patterns to classify unseen emails as either spam or not spam. As you already know, it doesn't always work right. However, every time you tell it that it's made a mistake, the algorithm learns. If you think about it, a decade ago, spam algorithms were wrong far more frequently than they are now. This is because every time someone marks an email as not spam or vice versa, the algorithm learns. Considering that hundreds of millions of people use the same email system (Gmail, for example), that's a lot of data for the algorithm to learn from.

Classification models can be used for other things, such as whether the value of a stock or commodity will rise or fall. They can also include more categories, so they don't have to be binary. For example,
if you want to figure out who will win a talent competition with multiple contestants.

Regression Models

Regression, on the other hand, is a predictive statistical process. In this case, the algorithm tries to determine important relationships between dependent and independent variables. The goal is for the algorithm to be able to forecast actual numbers, such as sales and income.

In other words, instead of trying to figure out if the value of a commodity will rise or fall, we want to figure out what the price will be in seven days. Or, instead of determining whether a student will fail or pass a test, we want to know what grade they'll get. Maybe instead of attempt-ing to figure out if the temperature this winter will be higher or lower, we want to know by how much. While these issues are related, they still represent different problems from their classification versions.

Most fields contain classification and regression problems. However, you must remember that these problems can be solved in multiple ways.
For example, let's say that you're a forex trader and you want to predict how the U.S. dollar will perform over the next few weeks so you can profit. You can use a classification model to figure out if it's going up or down, which will tell you whether to go short or long. However, you could also use a regression model for a more specific prediction, such as what price the EUR/USD will be trading at tomorrow.

In the first case, the situation is a little nebulous. While you might make a profit,
the risk is far greater than if you were to use a regression model, which will give you more information to make an effective decision.

The idea is that each approach will give you different types of information that will impact performance and, ergo, the strategy you employ.

Unsupervised Learning

In unsupervised ML, an algorithm will infer patterns from data without the benefit of a targeted or labeled outcome. This type of learning cannot be applied to classification or regression problems because you don't know what the output might be, making it impossible to train the algorithm like normal.

In other words, unsupervised learning is all about the algorithm learning from data on its own and usually refers to clustering. This means that the training data you provide the algorithm only has inputs, without the desired outputs. Instead, the algorithm clusters the inputs based on the patterns it identifies. The system tries to find significant regularities that it can group. It involves no supervision.

With no guidance, this approach to ML can be challenging because the problems tend to be poorly defined. Unsupervised learning is effec-tive, though, in helping to determine the data's underlying structure. Also, human interpretation is generally necessary, at the very least close to the end of the pipeline.
Unsupervised learning can discover patterns you wouldn't have otherwise known about. However, the reality is that it's not as effective as supervised learning. Another factor that makes supervised learning more applicable to practical problems is that, with unsupervised learning, you have no way of figuring out the accuracy of the results.

Unsupervised learning is generally best used when you don't have any information related to the desired outcome. One such example would be determining the target market of a completely new product. However, if you want to know more about your existing target market, then you're better off using supervised learning.

That doesn't mean unsupervised learning doesn't have its place. Some ways you can apply unsupervised learning are for clustering, anomaly detection, association mining, and latent variable models.

Clustering

With clustering, you can categorize the data into groups based on their similarity. It's not an approach that's widely used for applications such as customer segmentation, though, because it tends to overestimate how similar the groups are and doesn't see the data points as separate entities.

The biggest issue is that these types of problems are generally not well defined. For example, if you give an algorithm a series of images of various animals, the resulting clustering might not be relevant to your needs.

These images can be clustered in several ways, such as by color, type of animal, or habitat. None of these approaches are technically wrong, but some might be more useful than others.

The effectiveness of the result depends mainly on what your goal is. Therefore, it's important to have a well-defined goal and to experiment until you get it right. The good news is that if you test various algorithms, in the end, you will find one that works.

Anomaly Detection

Anomaly detection is useful for finding unusual information in your data. If something is unusual or anomalous in the data set, these algorithms will find it.

These algorithms have a wide range of real-world applications, especially for things like spotting fraudulent transactions. They can also be used to spot spikes in sales of various products but are just as helpful in detecting hackers.

Association Mining

Association mining is often used for basket analysis because it effectively identifies items that appear together frequently in your data. It's often used to help determine correlations in transactional, sales, and even medical data.

Latent Variable Models

Latent variable models are used to make the data easier to analyze and come in during the preprocessing phase. These models are effective for doing things such as lowering the number of features in a set of data, also known as dimensionality reduction, or even splitting the data up into multiple components.

With dimensionality reduction, the goal is to group together large numbers of variables into a lower number of factors, making the data easier to interpret. One of the most widely used techniques is factor analysis.

An example is the Big Five Personality Inventory, which was developed by gathering data from a large number of people and applying factor analysis to group the answers into five overall factors. Based on the Big Five personality theory, our personalities can be categorized as:

- Extraversion
- Agreeableness
- Conscientiousness
- Neuroticism
- Openness to experience

However, each of these major factors is made up of a wide range of variables. For example, an extroverted personality is characterized by friendliness, cheerfulness, assertiveness, and much more. Dimensionality reduction can be applied to many other problems, including user demographics and customer data.

Reinforcement Learning

Many experts believe reinforcement learning to be one of the keys to unlocking real AI because of the vast potential it holds. Moreover, it is growing at an accelerated pace and producing a wide range of algorithms for various applications.

Reinforcement learning is based on a punishment/reward system. It's a little like training your pet pooch. If you want to teach Fido to sit on command, you'll give him the command, show him what you want, and reward him with a treat. For a while, you continue to reward him every time he gets it right to reinforce the behavior.

When Fido doesn't listen to you, you usually have to repeat what you want until he does it and then reward him. Not receiving a reward is generally "punishment" enough for him to get that he's done wrong.

With an algorithm, things work slightly differently, but in essence, they are the same. For example, let's consider a robot learning to walk. If the step it takes is too long, it loses its balance and tips over. That's the punishment. So, it will keep changing the length of its step until it can move without falling over, which is the reward.

Or consider the same robot attempting to navigate a maze. Things are a little more complex here because it's not just an immediate solution. In the previous example, adjusting the length of the step will yield immediate results. With a maze, the first few steps might be right, until it reaches a dead-end and has to backtrack until it finds open space.

You might be wondering what the point is. Well, consider some real-world applications. Reinforcement learning is used for such things as driverless cars, robot vacuum cleaners, and more. Without reinforcement learning, your vacuum cleaner would keep slamming into the same obstacle instead of backing up to move around it.

Reinforcement learning is the closest thing to learning like a human.

Consider that any skill you learn and develop is based on experience.

Therefore, the more you practice, the better you get. However, it all boils down to reward/punishment. You've learned by discovering what works and what doesn't. Consider chess. The more you play, the better you get. That's because you amass more and more experience on what works and what doesn't in different situations. Reinforcement learning for machines works much the same way, which is why so many consider it to have so much potential. It allows for the resolution of very complex problems in a variety of environments.

Deep Learning

Deep learning studies neural networks that have multiple layers, also known as deep neural networks. A neural network is made up of neurons and the pathways that connect them, a bit like a connect-the-dots picture. The human brain is the most powerful computer that exists, so it makes sense for us to model artificial computers on something that already works so well.

In deep learning, artificial neural networks are used to help machines learn more quickly, more effectively, and at far greater volumes. It has been used to solve various problems that were believed to be unsolvable, such as natural language processing (NLP), speech recognition, and computer vision. At a very basic level, the way it works is that the input is generated from observation, which is then added to a layer. That layer generates an output, which becomes the input for the following layers until you get to the final output.

For example, when you look at a picture of an eggplant, you know it's an eggplant. But how do you know it's an eggplant and not an airplane or a basketball?

Your eyes see a specific shape and a specific color, and, based on experience, it translates those inputs into an abstract concept you understand. All this information is filtered from your eyes through multiple layers until it becomes an eggplant rather than an airplane.

Software applications such as Siri, Cortana, or Dragon Naturally Speaking can all understand you because of deep learning. It's also what allows these applications to learn and improve the more they interact with you.

This also applies to image or song recognition. Want to find out what a specific song is? Just get your app to listen to it, and it will be able to identify it. Likewise, want to find a particular item you can see in the real world? Take a photo of it, and the app will find it for you online.

Deep learning can also be used to generate language. OpenAI's GPT-3 is a very impressive model that can create articles so realistic that it is practically impossible to figure out how a machine writes them.

Another application for deep learning is that it has given computers the ability to identify different subjects in an image, such as being able to tell that chickens, horses, cats, and humans are different things.
It's also being used in things like graphic design, with plugins and apps that can remove backgrounds from photos while maintaining the full integrity of the subject. If you've ever tried to remove a background, you know how difficult it can be.

If it's not something you've attempted, then trust us when we say that, before deep learning enabled the creation of these apps, you needed a lot of time and patience. Even then, you still weren't guaranteed to get a result as good as these apps can offer in a fraction of the time.

It's a bit like the difference between hand painting one of those eggs with highly complex designs and painting your bedroom wall with a spray gun.

In conclusion, deep learning has allowed us to achieve some incredible things with machines and will continue to do so. Some believe that it might lead us to true AI, whereas others say that progress has plateaued. The big question for AI researchers is: what comes after deep learning? Only time will tell.

Other Types of ML

Quite a few other types of ML exist, including recommender systems, NLP, active learning, semi supervised learning, and weak supervision.

Recommender systems are designed to predict user interest and make recommendations accordingly. These are some of the most powerful ML systems used by retailers online to boost sales (Rodriguez 2018).
Consider Amazon, which has an excellent recommender system. Every time you log in, Amazon will recommend products or books they think you might like based on previous purchases and visits.

Spotify or Netflix use similar data to make recommendations in terms of the content you might enjoy. For example, if you watch a lot of action movies and crime dramas, then Netflix will recommend similar films and TV shows.

In ML, Natural Language Processing and text analytics involve the use of algorithms and AI to understand text, which can range from Facebook comments and online reviews to e-mails and regulatory documents (Barba 2020).

Active learning refers to the process of prioritizing data that must be labeled, so it has the highest impact on training a supervised model (Solaguren-Beascoa 2020).

Semi Supervised learning combines supervised and unsupervised ML methods so that an algorithm learns from data sets that include labeled and unlabeled data ("Semi-Supervised Machine Learning" n.d.).

Weak supervision or weakly supervised learning comprises a variety of approaches, including:
· Inexact supervision, where the training data is provided with only coarse-grained labels;
· Incomplete supervision that features data sets with only one subset that has labels;
· Inaccurate supervision, where the labels
aren't always ground truth (Zhou 2018).

For Decision Makers: How to Use Machine Learning

Machine learning really shines in cases where automation or prediction are needed. Irrespective of the actual form of ML being used in most cases, it is applied to the following cases:

1. Humans are performing a repetitive task, which also allows them to label data. The labeled data can then be used to train a ML model to replace the human. The most prominent example of this is computer vision and applications such as face recognition or recognizing certain entities in a photo (e.g., humans vs animals).

2. Predicting something about the future or an unknown quantity: credit scoring, spam detection, forecasting, customer churn all are viable applications of ML.

Understanding when and how to apply ML is a skill that takes a long time to master. However, a decision maker can just use the aforementioned heuristics to get a feeling of when they could use it. What is more important from a decision maker's perspective is making sure that there is a data strategy in place that can facilitate the use of ML. This is covered in the next chapter.

A Brief Intro to Statistics for the Decision Maker

Statistics is one of the core fields of data science. It was the first discipline to deal with data collection and analysis in a systematic way. In this section we will provide a brief overview of that area, as it can help us better understand the domain of data science.

Statistics is the study of how to collect, organize, analyze, and interpret numerical information and data. It encompasses both the science of uncertainty and the technology of extracting information from data.

It is a vital tool for any data scientist and is used to help us make decisions. This field employs a variety of methodologies that enable data scientists to do a variety of things, including:

· Design experiments and interpret results to improve product decision making;
· Develop models to predict signals;
· Mold data into insights;
· Understand a wide range of variables, including engagement, conversions, retention, leads, and

data science. While the discipline of statistics cannot be considered an emerging field (since it has been around for more than 200 years), it has found new uses in the era of big data.

Many data science applications, which could be considered emerging tech, are based on simple applications of statistics. Therefore, getting a good understanding of the basic uses of statistics can help put things into perspective as to how technologies and methodologies evolve and adapt as technology advances.

A Little History About Statistics

Statistics is a branch of mathematics dating back to approximately the 18th century. It was humanity's first attempt to analyze data systematically and is at the base of modern data analysis. It led to the development of summary statistics, regression classification, significant testing, forecasting, and more. Some prominent individuals in this field include Ronald Fisher, Karl Pearson (and his son Egon Pearson), and Jerzy Neyman.

Statistics is different from other data analysis fields because it focuses more on the theoretical soundness of the models and has traditionally dealt with smaller samples. This is mainly due to historical reasons because data had to be collected in person until relatively recently. It's only since the advent of the Internet that we can collect data remotely, allowing for much larger sample sizes.

As you can imagine, collecting data in person was not only expensive but also time-consuming, which meant that small sample sizes were the norm. Furthermore, until computers became part of our lives, calculations had to be done manually. While the results were extrapolated to the entire population using a margin of error, those calculations still took time. Today, solving a model might take seconds, but in the 18th century, it would've taken days or weeks.

There's also a different mentality when it comes to statistics. As this field is rooted in math, it is very strict on model assumptions and development. These assumptions must be validated and verified before you can do anything else. On the other hand, in ML, the goal is to achieve the objective and ask questions later.

One crucial difference between ML and statistics, for example, is that ML has led to impressive performance, even though statistics is far more transparent and has a higher degree of interpretability. The thing is that the high-level performance ML offers means that we've been able to achieve things that were previously thought impossible.

While some statisticians are completely against ML because of the reduced level of transparency and lack of theory, the fact is that statistics and ML work hand-in-hand. They are also both tools the data scientist can and should use depending on the situation. In other words, if you want interpretability, then you should turn to statistics. On the other hand, if you're looking for performance and predictive power, then ML is the way to go.

A Short Intro to Statistics

Statistics can be split into two branches: descriptive and inferential statistics.
Descriptive statistics is what most people consider statistics to be. It involves collecting data, using summary metrics such as the name and data visualization.

On the other hand, inferential statistics is what most people in the field consider to be statistics. It involves more advanced concepts such as sampling and inferring values of the population parameters.

Descriptive Statistics

Descriptive statistics involves organizing, summarizing, and presenting data so everyone can understand and make use of it. To do this, there are two sets of methods, namely numerical methods to describe data and graphical methods for data presentation ("Understanding Descriptive and Inferential Statistics | Laerd Statistics" n.d.).

Inferential Statistics

Inferential statistics represents the majority of the field because that's where the work is really done, while descriptive statistics represents a tiny fraction.

Inferential statistics comprises a group of methods you can use to draw conclusions or inferences about the traits of a whole population based on sample data.

In essence, inferential statistics allows you to quantify uncertainty. So, for example, let's say that you want to figure out something about a group of people. It could be something like the average age of the population.

If you were dealing with a small population, say maybe a few hundred people, then you could measure everyone's age and calculate the average. However, when you try to do that for an entire country, for example, that might have a population of 20 million people, it will be practically impos-sible. Well, at least unfeasible from a cost and effort viewpoint.

So, if studying every individual is impractical, there must be an alter-native. That's where inferential statistics comes in. It involves taking a sample of the population you are attempting to study and expressing uncertainty through probability distribution. You're essentially turning uncertainty into a quantifiable metric, which then allows you to run calculations. That is what permits statistical modeling and hypothesis testing. quantifiable metric, which then allows you to run calculations. That is what permits statistical modeling and hypothesis testing.

What you do is take a sample of a thousand people, which covers as wide a demographic as possible and then extrapolate their average age to the entire population of 20 million. While demographic conformity is not absolutely necessary, it does lead to more accurate results.

For example, consider deaths caused by the coronavirus. There were many conversations over the first few months of the pandemic about the actual mortality rate of the disease. Many disagreements arose between statisticians. At least some of those deaths attributed to COVID-19 were caused by other conditions. Still, at the same time, some covid-re-lated deaths, especially before tests became available, were attributed to other illnesses. This is a classic problem of inferential statistics: trying to decipher the value of an underlying variable, given a sample.

Another interesting inferential issue around COVID-19-related deaths is related to definitions and attribution. Let's say someone had severe underlying conditions and would probably die within the next month. If this person died and then tested positive for COVID-19, was the illness the cause of death or the underlying conditions?

The topic of attribution raises more of a philosophical discussion and is encountered in many health-related discussions. For example, who is the true culprit of the obesity epidemic? The companies selling unhealthy food, the advertisers, or the people buying it? While many people will have strong opinions on the subject, it is difficult to attri-bute this phenomenon to a single factor completely. This is where inferential statistics can help provide more clarity by quantifying each factors' contribution.

The Benefits of Statistics

All this might sound very interesting, but you're probably wondering how statistics can help you in business as a decision maker.

First, you're probably already using descriptive statistics in some shape or form. Profit and loss forecasts are just one example of using statistics in a business setting.

Inferential statistics, on the other hand, can be used to answer specific questions regarding the importance of a variable. It can also answer ques-tions about differences in population.

The main things you'll be using inferential statistics for are hypothesis testing and statistical modeling. While forecasting is another beneficial area, it is somewhat more technical, and it can often be achieved using ML more easily than through statistics.

Hypothesis testing is generally used for finding out the value of a population parameter or making comparisons.

Working out the value of a population basically means that you are looking to determine the specific value, such as average height, average income, and average age. Comparisons involve analyzing the differences and/or similarities among parameters. One example would be exploring differences based on gender. So, you would look at whether men earn more or less money in a specific job than women.

In business, especially online, you might have already heard of A/B testing, which is a form of comparison. So, when you test two calls-to-action against each other to determine which generates the highest conversion rate, you are conducting a comparison-based hypothesis test. Statistical modeling is what you use when you want to figure out if one variable affects another.

So, let's say you've conducted your comparison-based hypothesis test on your calls-to-action to determine which is more effective at achieving conversions. You've established which one is more successful, but you also want to learn testing and statistical modeling. While forecasting is another beneficial area, it is somewhat more technical, and it can often be achieved using ML more easily than through statistics.

Hypothesis testing is generally used for finding out the value of a population parameter or making comparisons.

Working out the value of a population basically means that you are looking to determine the specific value, such as average height, average income, and average age. Comparisons involve analyzing the differences and/or similarities among parameters. One example would be exploring differences based on gender. So, you would look at whether men earn more or less money in a specific job than women.

In business, especially online, you might have already heard of A/B testing, which is a form of comparison. So, when you test two calls-to-action against each other to determine which generates the highest conversion rate, you are conducting a comparison-based hypothesis test. Statistical modeling is what you use when you want to figure out if one variable affects another.

So, let's say you've conducted your comparison-based hypothesis test on your calls-to-action to determine which is more effective at achieving conversions. You've established which one is more successful, but you also want to learn what other variables could be affecting your conversion rate.

To do so, you would use statistical modeling.

Essentially, you plug in your variables into the model and may dis-cover that everything. from the button's position on the page and the color of the text to the headline and content, affects conversion rates. You can also determine to what degree these variables affect conversion rates. For example, you might find that the headline and call-to-action play only a small part in why people are converting and that the main draw is the offer itself.

Applications of Statistics in Business and Economics

In today's digital world, we have vast amounts of statistical data available to us at our fingertips. The most effective business leaders and decision makers are aware of the value of this data and can use it effectively. Here are some of the applications of statistics in business:

Accounting

Accounting companies often use statistical sampling methods when they conduct audits for clients. For example, let's say that an accounting company wants to figure out if the accounts receivable on the client's
balance sheet accurately represents the total amount of accounts receivable (Dilip n.d.).

Large corporations often have significant numbers of individual accounts receivable, which makes it far too time-consuming and expensive to validate each entry. Thus, the audit team will often select a sample of those accounts and, after reviewing and validating them, the auditors will conclude whether the amount on the balance sheet is accurate or not.

Finance

Financial analysis involves the use of a lot of statistical information to help investors make decisions. For example, Forex trading relies on the analysis of financial data, including historical price movement, a country's economic data, and much more. It also involves using a wide range of indicators that are calculated using statistical information, such as the moving average.

The same applies to stocks, where investors make decisions on which stock to invest in based on variables such as price/earnings ratios and dividend yields. Some might even conduct a comparison between the market average and the results of an individual stock.

Marketing

Statistics is also highly useful in marketing. Electronic scanners at retail checkout counters collect data for various marketing research applications. AC Nielsen, an information supplier, purchases this data from grocery stores, then processes it and sells statistical summaries to manufacturers and distributors, among others.

Companies will spend a lot of money to obtain this kind of data because it can be used to determine production necessities and even assist in developing new products.

Production

Quality control is an essential application of statistics in manufacturing. Various statistical quality control charts are used to monitor the output of the manufacturing process, such as an x-bar chart, which can be used to monitor average output.

For example, let's say that a machine fills containers with 1.5 ounces of cream. Sporadically, an employee will select a sample of containers and calculate the average number of ounces in the sample. This average value is then plotted on an x-bar chart.

A plotted value above the upper control limit indicates that the machine is overfilling the containers, whereas a plotted value below the lower control limit indicates underfilling. The process continues as long as the plotted value falls between the upper and lower control lim-its. Otherwise, adjustments are made to ensure the average is where it should be.

Economics

Economists frequently predict the future of the economy or certain aspects of it. They use a variety of statistical information to make these predictions, such as forecasting GDP, inflation rates, and more. However, these predictions are often made using ML.

Information Systems

Information systems administrators handle the daily operations of the company's computer networks. They use various statistical information to assess performance and make adjustments to ensure that the system is functioning optimally.

The Pitfalls of Statistics

One of the biggest problems with statistics is that people tend to trust them blindly simply because they appear to be facts. After all, when some-one presents you with information, and it's backed by what looks like accurate data in the form of numbers, ratios, percentages, graphs, charts, and so on, you're far more likely to believe what you're being told.

However, it is very easy to use statistics to lie to people. While it's not always a matter of bad intentions, even human error can lead to skewed results, which can cause problems.

Therefore, it's essential that you understand how statistics can be used to distort facts. This way, you will be more aware and less likely to make poor decisions because you've been misled. Here are some of the ways in which you can be lied to using statistics:

Lying Using Charts

One way statistics can be used to mislead an audience is by lying to people using charts that contain spurious correlations. They seem to make sense at first glance, but have no connection one to another.

For example, here is one chart that correlates the divorce rate in Maine with the per capita consumption of margarine (Figure 6.2).
Here's another chart that attempts to correlate worldwide noncommercial space launches with sociology doctorates awarded in the United States (Figure 6.3). Now, these might seem like interesting statistics and, separately, they certainly are. However, when you try to establish a correlation between these facts, it's a bit ridiculous.

For example, the first chart seems to imply that as divorce rates decline in Maine, so too does the consumption of margarine. Some enterprising individuals might attempt to convince you that margarine has affected the divorce rate, and the less margarine people eat, the less likely they are to get a divorce. The second chart seems to imply that an increase in sociology doctorates has led to a rise in the number of worldwide noncommercial space launches. Now, you might scoff and say that it's quite obvious there are no correlations between these variables. After all, how can the number of sociology doctorates awarded in the United States affect space launches? However, what happens is that people use variables that might seem to have a tangential connection to each other to attempt to convince you that a spurious correlation is fact.

A spurious correlation means that someone is trying to correlate two variables that don't really have an underlying theory that holds up to scrutiny. They are simply comparing two variables that aren't connected.

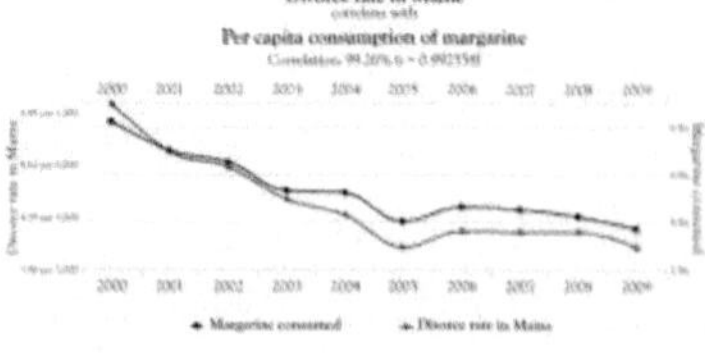

Figure 6.2 Divorce rate in Maine
Sources: National vital statistics reports and U.S. department of agriculture

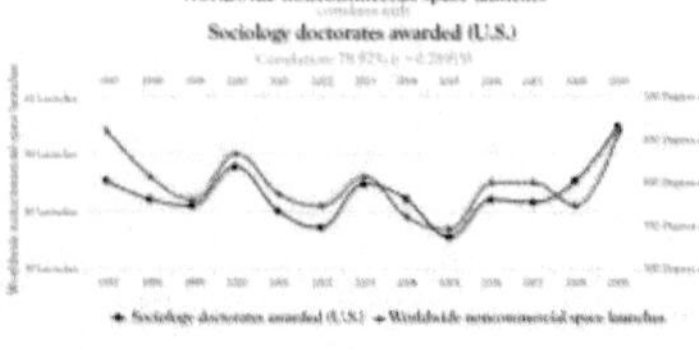

Figure 6.3 Worldwide noncommercial space launches
Source: Federal aviation administration and national science foundation

Furthermore, it's important to remember that correlation doesn't necessarily imply causation. For example, the consumption of margarine is in no way related to the number of divorces in Maine.

After all, it's not like a spread can have such an impact on people's relationships. You might go so far as to say that an argument over margarine led to a divorce. However, if people are arguing over margarine so much that they end up divorcing, there are many other underlying issues, and margarine is only an excuse rather than a cause.

However, if we were to attempt to correlate the consumption of margarine and income in the margarine industry, then the correlation would make sense because the two are connected. In some charts, people can be tricked even more because things like reversing the X- and Y-axis can lead to mistaken conclusions.

For example, suppose the numbers along the X-axis decrease while those on the Y-axis increase. In that case, this will lead to an erroneous visual representation, which is another way to attempt to force a correlation.

So, just remember that even if there might seem to be a significant correlation between two variables, that doesn't actually mean there is a relationship between the two.

Another way you can be lied to with charts is by using different types of scales in the same chart. For example, you can use different scales to make items seem as if they're closer to each other.

Another way to lie is to change the scale. If you close in on the scale, a variable's evolution might seem choppy. However, when you zoom out, it looks far more stable.

For example, if you take a snapshot of last year's performance of the Dow Jones industrial index (simply google "Dow Jones chart") you will see that growth has stalled (Figure 6.4). But if you look at a multidecadal chart, you will see that the index has been rising over the long run (Figure 6.5). An analyst who focuses on recent developments might get worried, while someone focused more on the long run can be reassured that the economy will simply keep growing. Graph interpretation can be quite subjective at times, and this is why a decision maker must always be skeptical and critical of any graph interpretations.

Embellishing With Descriptive Statistics

Descriptive statistics can also be used to mislead people, and one way to do so quite easily is through measures of centrality and summary metrics.

You have three main measures of centrality: the median, the mode, and the mean.

The mean represents the average of a set of numbers, which is basically where you add all the numbers together and divide the result by the number of variables you added together. The median is the central value in a list of numbers, and the mode is the value that shows up most frequently in a list.

If a distribution is symmetrical, these three values will fall on the same point. However, if the distribution is positively skewed, the mean will be lighter than the median, and the median will be lighter than the mode. If the distribution is negatively skewed, then the opposite happens.

It's important to note this because most distributions in life aren't symmetrical. For example, let's say that a company pays its CEO $300,000 per year, while the rest of the 10 employees earn $50,000 per year each.

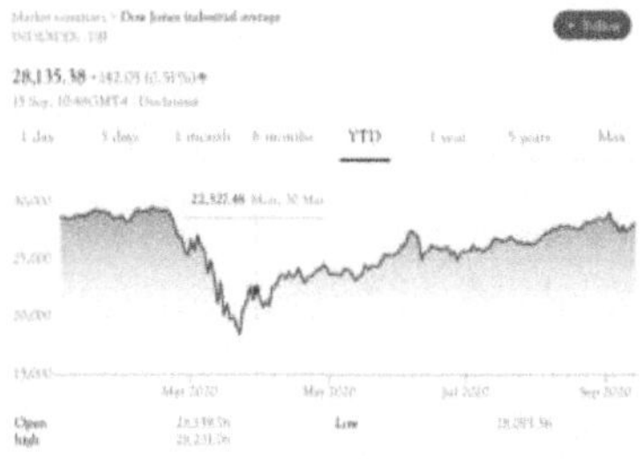

Figure 6.4 Dow Jones industrial index for 2020

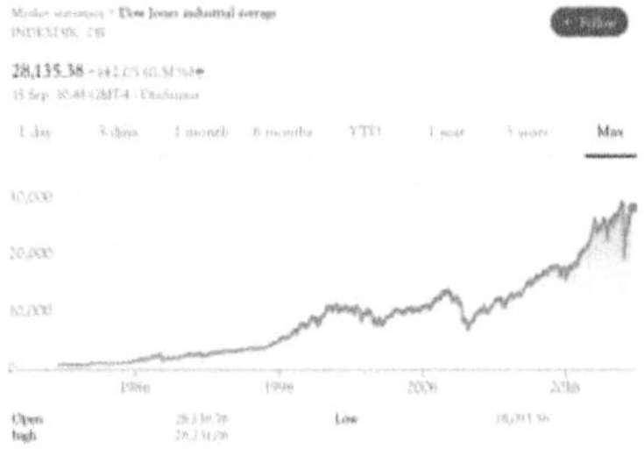

Figure 6.5 Dow Jones industrial index long-term trend

Depending on what you want to achieve, you can present different numbers. In this case, the median might be $50,000 per year, but the mean is $72,000 per year.

A company could advertise the mean figure, which would make people think that that's what they could earn, but the company is unwilling to pay more than $50,000 per year for anybody other than the CEO.

This way, they could trick potential employees into accepting a job because they believe they will eventually earn $72,000, when in fact, they'll never receive more than $50,000. It might seem underhanded—it is, in case you were wondering—but not as unusual as you might think.

Sampling Biases. Sampling biases can also lead to less than accurate data that can cause problems in the decision-making process. While there are quite a few different sampling biases, we will be looking at five: the selection bias, the area bias, the self-selection bias, the leading question bias, and social desirability bias, as they are the most common in business.

Two very famous cases of sampling bias are the forecasting of the Brexit vote in Britain and the 2016 presidential election in the United States. The forecasters in both cases got it completely wrong, because of bias that got introduced into the sample and completely invalidated most statistical models that were used (Kampakis 2016).

Selection Bias. The selection bias is the most significant. In fact, the other types of bias can actually be seen as related or even as subcategories of selection bias.

Selection bias occurs when the sample being used is not representative of the whole. Something is going on that ensures the subjects or items in the sample are special somehow, while other subjects are left out. One interesting example of selection bias is the attempt of the U.S. government to increase the survival rate of U.S. aircraft during the Second World War.

The initial attempt was conducted after investigators analyzed planes that had survived. The recommendation was to add more armor to the areas that had received the most amount of damage. When the armor was mounted, instead of leading to a higher rate of survivability, the exact opposite happened. The extra armor made the planes heavier, slower, and far less agile, making it easier for the enemy to destroy them. Further-more, the aircraft that survived still had significant amounts of damage in the same areas.

The government turned to Abraham Wald, who was a statistician. He realized that selection bias was taking place. In other words, instead of looking at what was important, the investigators made their decisions based on planes that had survived the damage they received.

That's when Wald concluded that the areas that required protection were actually the areas that were sensitive and hadn't been damaged. Once those areas were reinforced, survivability increased (Mangel and Samaniego 1984).

This is an interesting way that you can use statistics without even con-ducting any significant analysis. Wald had to understand that selection bias was taking place, which allowed them to fix the problem.

Area Bias. Area bias refers to attempting to generalize results from one area to another. This poses many problems, especially when you're trying to cross cultures.

For example, if you conduct marketing research in the United States, and you attempt to apply the results to another area, such as the Middle East, you're going to have a big surprise. The cultural, financial, lingual, and many other differences will have a significant impact, basically making those results null and void.

Self-Selection Bias. Self-selection bias refers to the increased likelihood of a person deciding to participate in a study because of traits they already have. For example, if you conduct a study on using makeup, you are more likely to get people participating in the survey who use makeup frequently than those who don't at all or do so rarely.

The problem is that this leads to a non-representative sample. Of course, this depends on what you're attempting to achieve. However, if you want the sample to be truly representative, you need to talk to people who use makeup and who don't use makeup or use it rarely.

Leading Questions Bias. A very easy way to get the answers you want rather than the truth is to use leading questions in your questionnaires. For example, if you ask someone if they believe teachers aren't paid enough and the answers you provide them are:

(a) Yes, they should earn more;

(b) No, they should not earn more;

(c) No opinion.

Most people will say A; teachers should definitely be paid more. This is because people want to be nice and provide what seem like socially acceptable answers. Plus, the way the question was phrased only really gives them one option.

Social Desirability Bias. Social desirability bias occurs when people want to paint themselves in a better light, which is almost always. So, if you pose questions about social desirability issues, your data will be skewed because nobody wants to admit they don't fall in line with societal expectations. So, for example, if you ask someone how frequently they donate to charity, or how often they recycle, or how much food they throw away, you are unlikely to receive accurate answers. If someone tells you that they only throw out 3 percent of the food they buy, they are probably not telling the truth since throwing away food is not exactly considered socially acceptable as it's a massive waste. So, they will provide an answer they feel is more socially acceptable instead of the truth.

Lying With Inferential Statistics

Some believe that it's impossible to lie with inferential statistics. Unfortunately, that's not exactly accurate. It might be challenging to lie with inferential statistics, but it can still be done.

These takes place a lot in research. When testing a hypothesis, you'll get a p-value. This value needs to be below a certain threshold for the tests to have statistical significance. Generally speaking, this threshold is 0.05.

A theory says that a significant number of research papers have p-values that are unusually close to 0.05. In other words, the results of these papers seem significant, but only by a tiny margin, because the value of p is just below 0.05, allowing them to meet the condition of the statistical significance.

The theory in question says that this is being done on purpose. Academia is a very competitive environment, and people have to publish papers, or they'll end up without a job. So, people are basically under pressure to make the results look as if they are statistically significant. One way to achieve this is by conducting multiple experiments until you get the results you want.

Another way to do this is by massaging the data. However, in other cases, you can find research where the results are significant, but this is only because the model assumptions aren't being met and not because the researcher intended to deceive.

Case Studies and Examples

Here are some examples where data science can make a significant impact on business.

Preventive Maintenance Becomes Predictive Maintenance

Preventive maintenance is a key aspect of business for many firms across a wide range of industries because of the reduction of unplanned down-time. The latter can negatively affect the bottom line, which is why preventive maintenance is so valuable.

Like with any other aspect of business, improving maintenance efficiency is a big priority for many firms, especially those that rely on a lot of expensive machinery. Companies operating in industries such as manufacturing, shipping, oil and gas, rail, and freight can all benefit.

The goal of regular maintenance is to minimize failures, maximize the life of a machine, and ensure optimal performance and efficient operation.

The most common approach is for firms to use a maintenance schedule based on recommendations made by the manufacturer of the equipment or vehicles. It's just like with your car, where the manufacturer recommends you change the oil after 10,000 miles, for example.

This isn't a bad approach at all. It's certainly better than guessing or waiting for something to break down. However, it isn't ideal because failures still happen. The fact is that no one can plan for every situation and predict every issue.

For example, a manufacturer might recommend that you change fuel filters every 5,000 hours of operation, but that's in ideal operating conditions. If the diesel hasn't been the best quality or the machine is operating in very dusty or sandy conditions, the change will need to come sooner unless you want a lot of other problems to occur.

Avoiding unplanned downtime due to failures and breakdowns is essential because this downtime can be very expensive. It leads to a significant loss of revenue through lost output and reduced productivity.
The better alternative is planned downtime because you can plan to conduct maintenance at a time when the machine being inoperable will cause the least amount of problems. The key is figuring out when that is.

Many firms are turning to data and predictive analytics to solve their issues with maintenance scheduling (Kampakis 2020a).

In manufacturing, for example, the sensors on a production line can collect almost any information you need. You can then store and analyze the data. Algorithms can then use the data to determine when a failure might occur.

This process is referred to as predictive maintenance.

The predictive maintenance algorithms being used at the moment are usually based on ML, so their accuracy improves as they get better at identifying situations when failures are possible.
Furthermore, the whole process can be automated, which means that predictive analytics can work out when maintenance is necessary to avoid failure. It can also determine the best time for maintenance to occur to ensure it is the least disruptive, based on a variety of factors such as demand. Predictive maintenance offers significant boosts in productivity, improves customer service, reduces costs, and improves profits. As Google trends show, it has become very popular and will continue to increase in popularity as more firms understand the benefits.

Using AI and Data Science to Fight COVID-19

Owing to the novel coronavirus dubbed COVID-19, the world is facing a crisis that no one thought could occur in the modern world. At the time of this writing, the death toll has almost reached one million on a global scale with a total of 31.4 million cases of infection, and the crisis is still ongoing, with many experts warning of a second wave of mass infections.

Many organizations have turned to AI and data science to help in this time of crisis (Kampakis 2020b). The White House and the Allen Institute for AI have released a database of 29,000 research articles on the coronavirus family. These articles have been modified to ensure they are machine-readable by NLP libraries.

Using AI, researchers hope they will be able to generate new insights from all the work that's already been done into understanding this virus family.

The data set has also been put up as a Kaggle challenge to take advantage of crowdsourcing to come up with new insights and possible solutions.

AI can also assist in detecting people who are very vulnerable to infec-tion and developing severe complications from the virus. Medical Home Network uses such a system to first address those patients who are most in need of medical care.

AI can also help to create vaccines. A team from Australia's Flinders University designed an AI that managed to develop a drug on its own for the first time. While the technology is still in its infancy and not much help fighting COVID-19, it could be vital for a future pandemic.

AI can also help to reduce the strain on health care networks, with chatbots replacing doctors to answer simple

questions. For example, Ask-Sophie helps patients determine whether they have a common cold or COVID-19 ("Check Your Symptoms | Medicare" n.d.).

Traditional predictive analytics can also help forecast the future. Researchers in Israel, for example, are relying on AI to predict when the next breakout might occur, so they are in a better position to pre-vent it. The Israelis don't have a large number of tests available, so they need to be careful how they use them. They are, therefore, handing out questionnaires daily and relying on data science to work out which clusters of people could be infected.

Hiring the Right Person

As it has become clear by now, data science is a big and convoluted field, primarily because it is an aggregation of different scientific disciplines. This means that there are many different types of data scientists, and hiring one can be a fairly complicated process, as backgrounds can vary. A ML specialist might have a very different skill set from a pure statistician. We are looking into the topic of hiring and managing data scientists in Chapter 8 later on.

Key Takeaways

- Data science is a term that aggregates many different fields. The core ones being AI, ML, and statistics.

- The most popular types of ML are supervised and unsupervised learning. There are other subtypes, such as active learning and recommender systems, which can be useful for certain types of businesses.

- Statistics is broken down into descriptive and inferential statistics. The most interesting applications (like statistical modeling) fall within the spectrum of inferential statistics.

- When working with statistical methods it's important to try and avoid potential biases that might creep into the data.

- Hiring and managing a data scientist is not always easy, because there are data scientists of many different backgrounds.

CHAPTER 7

Thinking Like A Data Scientist (Without Being One)

In this chapter, we're going to talk about how to think like a data scientist without being one. It's probably the most exciting and interesting chapter of the book, but also the most important because it translates very technical terms and ideas into English. It offers a great view into the technical world of The Data Science Process.

So, if I ask the question, **What is data science about?**

I'll receive different answers because, no surprise, different people have different opinions. For example, the boss might think that data science is actually a magical money machine that can print money whenever he or she wants it to. To customers, data science might make you seem like a wizard or a telepath or psychic because you can tell so much about them and solve so many of their problems. Software engineers think that data science is just importing some stuff from libraries and running a few functions, because of course no one is quite as awesome as they are.

In reality, though, data science is like an orchestra made up of different elements, including infrastructure, software, data sources, and statistics.

From a pragmatic point of view, there are five steps of a data science life cycle:

1. Collecting data
2. Organizing data
3. Analyzing data
4. Interpreting data
5. Communicating findings from data

We already covered collecting and organizing data in the previous chapters; therefore, we're going to look at steps 3–5 in this chapter and we'll cover the topics in enough depth so that you understand how it all works.Keep in mind, though, that data scientists are often called in from step 3 to step 5, because the collection and organization has already been done. Now, that doesn't mean it's always been done properly, but it has been done.

Defining the Data Science Process

The data science process has four steps, namely:

Step 1—Defining the problem.

Step 2—Choosing the right data

Step 3—Solving the problem

Step 4—Creating value through actionable insights

The process involves two main actors, namely, the domain expert and the data scientist. The domain expert is the person who owns the problem. It could be the business owner who hired the data scientist, but it could also be the head of a department that has to work with the data scientist. In an academic setting, it could be a researcher.

Essentially, the domain expert is the person who is responsible for solving the problem and who has to report either to himself (as a business owner or entrepreneur) or to upper management. It's also the person who knows all the specifics of the domain. Thus, the first step, namely, defining the problem, lies with the domain expert. Subsequently, choosing the right data is the responsibility of both actors, while the third step falls to the data scientist. Finally, creating value involves both actors working together.
So, let's take a closer look at all of these.

Step 1: Defining the Problem
So, the first step is to define the problem. Take something you find interesting at work. You could even decide to focus on something that bothers you.

I'm going to choose a trivial example, but one that most people can relate to, namely, meetings that consistently start late. The first thing to do is to frame the problem. A great trick is to turn the statement of the problem into a question and write it down. So, in our case, it would be
Meetings always seem to start late. Is that really true?

You want to take this approach because while most data scientists like concrete terms, most non-data scientists tend to think in terms that are vague. However, models, be they machine learning, statistical, or any other type, have a narrow focus and can answer one, two, or three specific questions. So, when you write down the problem as a question, it helps the data scientist develop a better model to reach the solution.

Step 2: Choosing the Right Data
This step will have two parts, namely, Part A where you think about the data and Part B where you collect the data.

Part A: Think About the Data
At this point, you need to consider what data you will require to answer the question you framed in Step 1. And then you have to decide how you will collect the relevant data. You start by writing down all the relevant definitions and thinking about the protocol you will use to collect the data. This is when the problems start, and you realize that even for simple problems there might be a wide range of different issues.

So, in our example, we want to study meetings that start late. To do this, though, we need to define when the meeting actually starts. It might seem simple at first, but if you really think about it, the definition isn't all that clear.
Thus, does the meeting start when someone says it's time to get started? Or is it the time the meeting was scheduled for in the calendar? Or is it when the actual work of the meeting starts—

you know, after all the chit-chat and inquiring about the boss' kids, dog, cat, hamster, and crocodile? Or is all that small talk that takes place in the first few minutes part of the meeting too? Some might think that bit is a waste of time, while others might find it important for relationship building.

It might seem pretty trivial, but all these things are important because things can go wrong. The main risk is that you use the wrong definitions and they prevent you from solving the problem.

For example, meetings might consistently start late because of small talk. However, when you wrote down the definition, you didn't factor in this small talk and, therefore, recorded a different time for the start of the meeting. So, you can't solve the problem because the cause is completely missing from the data. As a result, you have to go back and collect data again, thereby wasting time, energy, and resources.

Part B: Collect the Data

Now that you've defined your data, it's time to move on to the collection part of the project. The first thing to consider is that you need data you can trust, which can be more difficult than it sounds.

Data can suffer from a wide range of issues such as missing values, erroneous entries, definition issues, and much more. And these are pretty frequent problems.

We covered this in the previous section as well as how to prevent or fix these problems.

Due to these problems, it's a good idea to be flexible and adaptable. For example, it could be a good idea to modify your definition and the data collection protocol as you go along if things aren't progressing as they should.

So, come back to our meeting example. Let's say your initial definition doesn't include the "small talk" portion of the meeting. However, you realize it's extremely relevant since it delays the start of the actual meeting by approximately 30 minutes. Well, you can't solve the problem if the data doesn't show it exists, so you go back and change the definition but also how you collect the data.

What is vital, though, is that there is complete transparency and everything is documented regarding what you changed, how you changed, when you changed it, and so on. This is important because you could end up with situations like variables meaning completely different things but using the same terms to define them.

For example, let's say you don't document your decision to include small talk as part of the meeting. The time you record as the start time changes, but no one knows about it because you didn't document the change.

Then, you comb through the data with the data scientist, who can't figure out why nothing works properly.

The reason is, of course, that the variable referring to the start time has two different definitions depending on when it was recorded during the project, namely, before or after you made the change.

Effectively, you're dealing with two variables and not one, which can seriously mess up any statistical model. This is just one example of how things can go wrong when you don't document everything you are doing. Many more things can occur, leading to disastrous results.

As you aren't a data science expert, there's no way for you to foresee what problems might arise with the data, which is why you want to be fully transparent regarding what's going on and to document every tiny little thing that you do. Remember, you always want to make the data scientist's life as easy as possible because it will take them less time to get up to speed and it will enable him or her to develop a more effective solution, helping you save time and money while greatly improving efficiency and productivity.

Step 3: Solving the Problem
In this phase, there's not a lot you can do as the domain expert since it's mainly the data scientist's job. However, let's take a quick look at what this step usually entails anyway just so you can get an idea of what's going on.

Usually, most data scientists like to start by performing exploratory data analysis. They use summary metrics, graphs, and so on to gain a better understanding of the problem. In some cases, they might even present some early findings to the stakeholders.

So, in our example, a data scientist might say something like:
"Over a two-week period, 10% of the meetings started on time. On average, meetings started 12 minutes late." Or, he or she might discover that meetings usually started late when they covered topics X and Y and when certain people attended, like the manager who loves to tell everyone what he did over the weekend in minute detail and no one can seem to get him to stop talking.

The data scientist will then build a model to find a solution, but models are mainly used to answer specific questions.

You can have a primary question, which in our example could be
Are people usually late for meetings?

But you can also have a number of secondary ones. In our example, they could be along the lines of

- Does the subject being covered affect how long a meeting runs?
- Do the people in attendance have an effect on how late the meeting is?
- Are late meetings counterbalanced by meetings that finish early?
- What is the overall meeting time?
- Can you describe this in terms of a distribution?

Of course, all these questions are related and that means more than one can be answered. Keep in mind, though, that when you frame your problem as a question, you are helping the data scientist. He or she will be better able to understand how to convert vague data into a model that can be used to solve the problem.

Step 4: Creating Value Through Actionable Insights

By this point, the data scientist has built one or more models to answer the aforementioned questions, so we can move on to the final step, namely, to extract actionable insights from the models.

Essentially, the models are useless if you don't act on them. The first step to taking action is to understand the impact of the results. A good way to do that is to translate the findings into monetary terms.

In other words, if the time period studied for late meetings is typical, then each employee loses an hour per day, which costs the company $X per year. Another approach to understanding the impact of the results is by identifying specific individuals or culprits behind the problem.

So, in our example, we could say that person X is responsible for late meetings, so what can we do to solve the issue? Could we help them manage their time better? Would that help fix the problem? Based on this understanding you gain from the results, you can then take action.

It's also a good idea to go beyond the results, though. This cycle of modeling, translating the results, and then taking action can also be a very good learning experience for you. When you go through this process, other questions pop up. This is the point when some of those secondary questions mentioned in step 3 arise.

It also makes sense to build models for these secondary questions too since the data is already there and the data scientist has gained experience with the data. It pays to make the most out of the data.

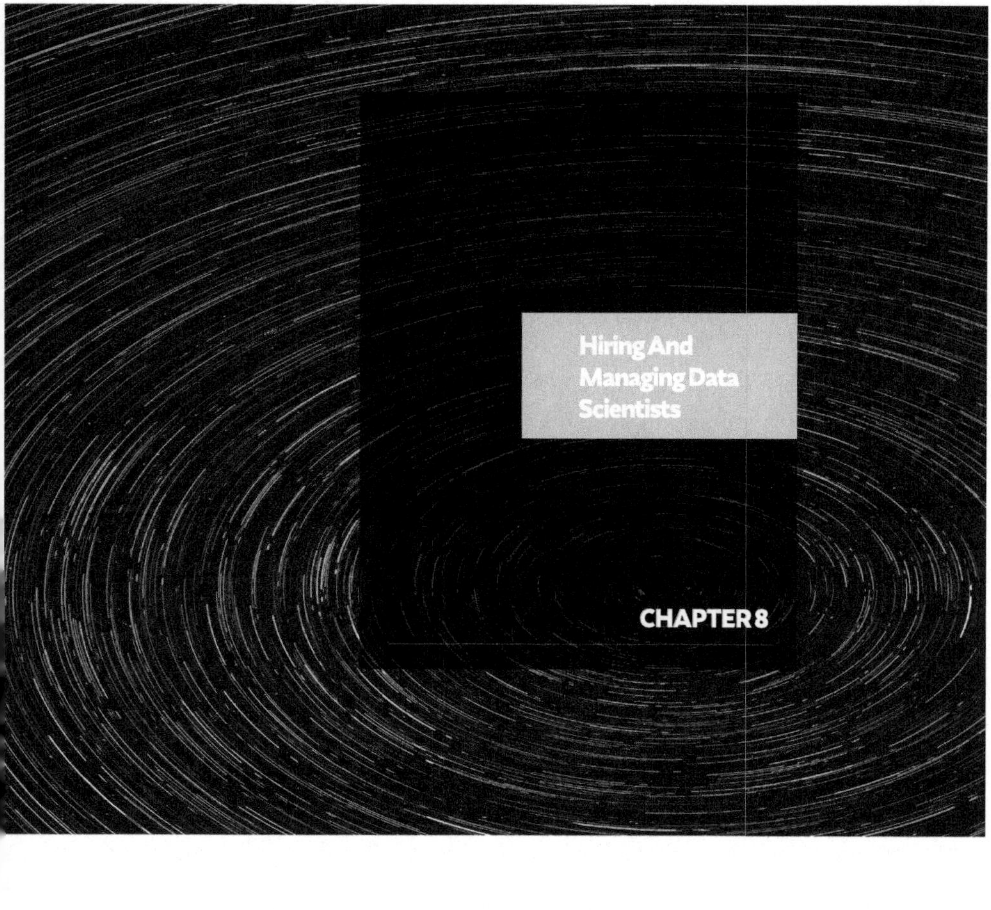

Hiring And Managing Data Scientists

CHAPTER 8

Hiring And Managing Data Scientists

We've talked about why you should hire a data scientist and the numerous benefits it will bring your business. We've also looked at why it's important to let them do their job without you trying to guide them. But to do that, you need to hire someone you can trust.

In this chapter, we'll be looking at precisely how to hire and manage a data scientist to get the best possible results. First, let's try to understand data scientists a little better.

Into the Mind of a Data Scientist

A competent data scientist needs to have a lot of knowledge and a wide range of skills, but certain skills are more important than others.

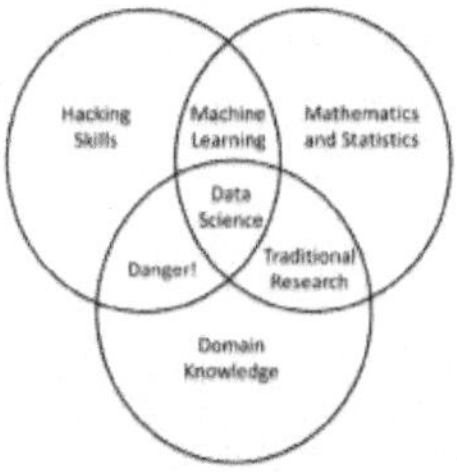

Figure 8-1. The data science Venn diagram

As you can see in Figure 8-1, a data scientist needs hacking skills, math and statistics knowledge, and substantive expertise. While each of the skills is highly valuable individually, if they only have two of the three, they are not a data scientist—and in one particular case, it can actually lead to problems.

Code Hacking Skills

Okay, so when I say code hacking skills, I'm not talking about breaking into NASA, but the fact is that a data scientist needs to have excellent computer knowledge and decent programming skills. This doesn't mean that they need a computer science degree as there are plenty of excellent "hackers" out there who have never taken a single computer course in their life.

However, a data scientist needs to be able to think algorithmically, understand vectorized operations, and work with text files at the command line. Without these skills, it's not possible to be a data scientist. In most cases, the actual quality of the code that data scientists produce does not have to be production level. That's why we are using the term code hacking, instead of software engineering, as the latter means the code should be of very high standard. Data scientists use the code as a tool in order to reach solutions to problems. However, it won't hurt if you find a data scientist whom might also have very good coding skills.

Mathematical and Statistics Knowledge

Once those hacking skills have been used to get the data into shape, it's time to analyze it and extract insights. For this, a data scientist needs to have math and statistics knowledge so they can apply the right methods and models.

Again, a data scientist doesn't need a PhD in statistics to be effective at their job, but they must know how to develop and work with mathematical and statistical models, including how to interpret the results.

Domain Knowledge

Domain knowledge is important for a data scientist: the need to understand the subject matter and not just the technical aspects of it. While this is not a hard requirement, lack of domain knowledge can cause all sorts of issues (we've already seen some examples, and more will follow). Domain expertise allows data scientists to apply the other skills to the data in such a way that they reach the desired goal. Data scientists have to teach themselves the peculiarities of a domain, every time they move to solving problems in a field they've not encountered before.

Two Is Not Enough

Only having two of these skills/knowledge is insufficient. A capable hacker with knowledge of math and statistics but no substantive expertise would be ideally suited for machine learning. However, their skills won't make them a data scientist.

Likewise, if someone has substantive expertise and knows math and statistics, then they are probably looking at traditional research. This intersection is basically what much of academia is made up of—though it should be noted that young researchers are choosing to evolve and learn more about tech. However, without those hacking skills, they will never be a data scientist.

The real problem arises when you have someone who is a skilled hacker and has substantive expertise. It creates a dangerous person because they know just enough to create what seems to be a legitimate analysis but they have no clue how they reached their conclusions or what they've actually created.

Essentially, these are people who have the skills to apply analytics on a problem, but lack the theoretical foundation to make sure they are doing the right thing. So, they might run a statistical test, but could be making erroneous assumptions. However, since they believe they are basing their decisions on data, they have a false sense of confidence which can lead to serious problems.

So, remember, a competent data scientist will be a skilled hacker, have math and statistics knowledge, and also have substantive expertise in your chosen field.

What Motivates a Data Scientist?

Working effectively with someone means understanding who they are and what motivates them. Unfortunately, it can be difficult for people to understand data scientists, precisely because they have such a wide range of skills that they can't be neatly slotted in a box.

A data scientist isn't just someone who knows math and statistics and can work a computer like a pro. These are people who also have great communication and visualization skills, enabling them to communicate well with senior management as well as to tell a story effectively.

They are also passionate about the business and curious about data. They constantly want to learn more and they want to solve problems and influence things without the authority that might usually accompany this role. They are strategic, proactive, creative, and innovative people who like to collaborate with others.

They definitely love to be mentally stimulated, and solving problems is their bread and butter. And they have an innate curiosity and drive to grow, which means they love learning new things and acquiring new skills.

The fact is that learning new skills is an integral component of today's market. It's the Red Queen's race or hypothesis in action, which essentially says that an organism must constantly adapt, evolve, and proliferate just to survive.

What Will Disengage a Data Scientist?

If you give your data scientist a lot of repetitive work, you are going to end up with a very disengaged person on your hands. So, if they have to spend ridiculous amounts of time cleaning up data or doing anything else that is the equivalent of counting grains of sand, you are going to be dealing with someone who really doesn't want to be there. And the results will suffer.

Likewise, if they get bored because the problems you are asking them to solve are too simple, you aren't going to win any points. Of course, sometimes simple problems need to be solved, but if you are going to make the leap and hire a data scientist, make sure to take full advantage of their capabilities. Otherwise, it would be like hiring a Michelin star chef to make you a grilled cheese sandwich. The peril is that the chef, out of boredom, will go off on a tangent and serve you a grilled cheese sandwich that's been deconstructed and reconstructed until it has little in common with that simple sandwich that you wanted.

Also, another problem stems from communication problems. Friction in communication often arises when upper management doesn't understand what the data scientist is doing.

A simple example is that the data scientist ends up doing a lot of data wrangling, which is utterly boring, because of bad communication with the developer in terms of how the data should have been stored.

To return to our Michelin star chef analogy, Heston Blumenthal is a world-renowned chef and his main "thing" is molecular gastronomy. He uses a range of tools and ingredients that are not always the norm in a kitchen. Say you hire him to cater for an event, and he tells you what he needs, but because you don't understand his process, you just stock the kitchen with all the usual tools and ingredients.

When he arrives to do the cooking, he ends up having to cook a traditional meal that is completely boring for him, resulting in food that might be decent but nowhere near the quality of what he could have done.

When a Data Scientist Is Looking for a Job

Right now it's a seller's market for good data scientists above junior level where the data scientists are the sellers—you know, seeing as they sell their skills and expertise. The fact is that there is a high demand for skilled people, but the supply is nowhere near sufficient to meet it.
For example, an average data scientist in London will receive between one and ten recruiter messages or calls every week.

This means they are in a position of power when choosing what projects to work on.
So, to improve your chances of hiring the right person, you need to understand what data scientists want.

What Does a Data Scientist Want?

The first thing is compensation, of course. After all, data scientists are human—even if their skillset and availability can make them seem akin to a mythological beast at times—and they not only need money to live, but they want their value to be appropriately compensated.
However, offering a mind-blowing paycheck alone will not be enough because other things matter too, such as the team they'll be working with, the problem they'll be tackling, the technology stack they'll be using, and the relationship to academia.

The Team

Some data scientists prefer to work in a team where they like the people they are working with. This usually means a geekier, less formal culture or even working from home.
Of course, this won't necessarily work for every company as you can't exactly change your whole culture overnight for the data scientist you are hiring, but you can try to make concessions where possible to improve the working relationship.

The Problem

While we've already discussed the dangers of giving to a data scientist problems that are too simple, you'll also find that many data scientists have a bias for particular types of problems. For example, some might prefer working on problems that have a social impact, while others might stick to problems in fields they like, such as medicine.

Other times, they might have preferences related to the problem itself. For example, some people prefer working with text data.
Often, though, you will find that it is closely connected to doing and learning something new, which is a trait that defines data scientists.

The Technology Stack

The technology being used will also play an important role. Some data scientists will prefer working with stacks they are already familiar with, while others will want to learn new things. However, you will find that most data scientists will avoid old technologies and legacy code like the plague. Sometimes learning new technologies can be extremely important to a data scientist. It could be because some up-and-coming technologies are dominating the landscape, like Python, and they might want to transition from MATLAB to Python and R, for example. Or maybe the data scientist wants to expand their skill set because some technologies offer better pay and are more interesting, such as those to do with deep learning.

Relationship to Academia

Many data scientists come out of academia and are used to reading/writing papers and going to conferences. This is an advantage for everyone because conferences can be an essential part of being on top of their game. So, one way to motivate a data scientist is to provide a stipend for conferences. And, as I already said, it will help you too because your data scientist will learn about the up-and-coming developments in data science, they will learn about fields or applications they weren't previously aware of, and they will catch up with other people in their field.

Some of the data science conferences you can expect a PhD-level data scientist to want to attend include

· ICML1
—The International Conference on Machine Learning
· NeurIPS2
—Neural Information Processing Systems
· SIGKDD3
—ACM SIGKDD International Conference on Knowledge Discovery and Data Mining
· ECML PKDD

—European Conference on Machine Learning and Knowledge Discovery in Databases
· AI Stats4

Avoiding Traditional Limitations

One frequent problem with hiring data scientists is that employers often take the same approach they would with hiring for any other role in the business. And that usually involves asking if the person has experience in a particular domain.

However, many data scientists, myself included, specifically seek out domains they have not worked in before. It's all about the drive to learn new things and stave off boredom because something you haven't done before will certainly prove more interesting than something you are experienced in.

The important thing that you, as a potential employer, need to understand is that the techniques a data scientist uses have general applicability and the domain itself is of secondary importance. In other words, don't miss out on hiring a great data scientist because they don't have experience in your particular domain.

Data Science Is a General Toolbox

The techniques in data science can be applied to a variety of problems. Experience in one thing can translate to experience in something else. So, for example, a data scientist might be able to use the same algorithms to predict disease outbreaks but also how many people might click on an ad.

Think of it like a pastry chef. They learn a wide range of techniques, including working with different kinds of dough, working with sauces, making creams, and so on. And they have a lot of experience making cakes. However, because they are highly experienced with the techniques, they can easily switch from making cakes to making pies.
For example, a common mistake I see made by human resources goes along the lines of

"We're looking for someone who has 5 years of experience in TensorFlow," says the HR department.

"Okay, but TensorFlow has only been around for 2 years," replies the candidate or even the recruitment firm.

When it comes to data scientists, their breadth of knowledge is generally a better indicator of their skills rather than just experience.

Let's look at a data scientist who works in finance as an example. In finances, data science would employ tools like time series and predictive modeling.

However, these tools aren't limited just to finances. They are equally effective for a number of other fields, such as in sports bettering or even retail. In retail, for example, you can use a time series to predict demand.

However, a large number of employers will see that the data scientist has experience in finance and will automatically assume his or her skill set is only applicable to finances. And this means they could be missing out on an amazing data scientist.
So, don't make the same mistake and give these people a chance, even if they don't conform to the strict model you have in your head of what the perfect hire would be.

Discovering Young Talent
Data science is a little like sports in that talent plays a huge role, especially because it requires a combination of technical skills and soft skills, as we've previously discussed. This person needs to be able to read other people, to make connections others can't see, and to communicate well, beyond the technical aspects of their skillset. They also have to be able to smoothly integrate their soft and technical skills, which isn't always as easy as it sounds.

So, when you find someone with a clear talent for this work, grab onto them with both hands, even if they are at the beginning of their career. Remember, someone who is a junior data scientist today can be your future senior data scientist if you give them a chance and nurture them.

How can you find young data scientists with talent? First, you want to check out the top universities teaching the subject. Then, once you've identified potential candidates, look beyond their university work. You can look on sites like GitHub5 to discover any outside work they've done. You should also consider creating a mentorship program. This will allow you to identify people with the talent for data science, some of whom you might not have realized have the aptitude for it until you work with them up close and personal.

A Few Typical Data Scientist Dilemmas
When it comes to data scientists, they are faced with a few dilemmas in terms of whom to work for. The options are a startup vs. a bigger company. Each comes with its own set of pros and cons.

First of all, there's the startup. When it comes to a startup, things will certainly be more interesting for a data scientist. They'll be dealing with new technologies and new problems, and they'll have a lot more flexibility. However, the downside is that they'll likely get paid less and stability can be an issue because, after all, many startups don't succeed.

Then you have big companies. The main advantages are that the paycheck will be much more impressive, as will the benefits package. There's also the matter of stability. A big company is unlikely to go belly up overnight and leave a data scientist in the lurch.

On the opposite end of the spectrum, though, the fact is that a data scientist might end up pulling out their hair in frustration because the work will be boring and as far from stimulating as you can get because they'll be dealing with old technology and legacy code, which they'll have to clean up. So, no, it's not going to be fun. At all.

Freeze Your Data Scientist Recruitment Drive Now

If your company isn't ready for data science, you need to stop trying to hire a data scientist. What does it mean to be ready for data science?

Well, first of all, you need to make sure your company has a data-driven culture in place. Everyone in your organization needs to understand the value of data, and they need to be willing to use it effectively.

If everyone thinks data is a waste of time or just something you're doing because it's the latest "fad," then you are going to waste your money and time hiring a data scientist.

Don't worry though, because a little later we're going to talk about how to build a data science culture, and you'll know exactly what you need to do.

The next consideration is whether or not you have the data available. If you haven't collected the data, then you might as well wait until you have it.

Otherwise, you'll be paying a data scientist to sit around and look pretty. It will also antagonize the data scientist because, as I've already mentioned, boredom is one of the things they hate the most. And a data scientist with nothing to work is a bored data scientist who will likely end up leaving your company faster than you can blink.

Lastly, you need to make sure the data scientist's work will have an impact. Just hiring someone to make data look pretty, so you can show off, but that's about it is a waste of resources. You need to make sure that you have a clear goal in mind—an important question that needs answering—or you'll be wasting your time and that of the data scientist's too.

When you do hire a data scientist, don't use them just as a highly sophisticated reporting tool. They are a lot more than that and you need to listen to their ideas and trust their recommendations. Don't make the mistake of thinking you know it all.

After all, would you tell your electrician how to rewire your house? Or would you tell your surgeon how to operate on you? Of course not. You'd let them do their jobs and take their advice because they're the experts. So, why would you do anything differently with your data scientist?

You also need to let them spread their wings. Don't freak out if they want to tackle the problem using a completely new approach. Just because it's not in line with what you had in mind doesn't mean it's not effective. In fact, trying something new is the best way to find the most effective solution.

Remember, doing the same thing over and over again and expecting different results is the definition of insanity. So, you need to give your data scientist the freedom to try something new.

Just put things a little more in perspective for you regarding why you shouldn't be hiring a data scientist if you're not ready; I remember a situation a while ago where a company hired a data scientist. However, the data scientist resigned after only 2 months, and they weren't happy when they did so.
What happened was that the company didn't have any data for the scientist to work on. They were still collecting it, but they jumped the gun, somehow thinking they needed a data scientist on board to look pretty while they were still gathering the information.

After all, would you tell your electrician how to rewire your house? Or would you tell your surgeon how to operate on you? Of course not. You'd let them do their jobs and take their advice because they're the experts. So, why would you do anything differently with your data scientist?

You also need to let them spread their wings. Don't freak out if they want to tackle the problem using a completely new approach. Just because it's not in line with what you had in mind doesn't mean it's not effective. In fact, trying something new is the best way to find the most effective solution.

Remember, doing the same thing over and over again and expecting different results is the definition of insanity. So, you need to give your data scientist the freedom to try something new.

Just put things a little more in perspective for you regarding why you shouldn't be hiring a data scientist if you're not ready; I remember a situation a while ago where a company hired a data scientist. However, the data scientist resigned after only 2 months, and they weren't happy when they did so.
What happened was that the company didn't have any data for the scientist to work on. They were still collecting it, but they jumped the gun, somehow thinking they needed a data scientist on board to look pretty while they were still gathering the information.

In terms of the major tribes, we have the **computer scientist**, the **statistician**, and the **quantitative specialist** who hails from some other field.

The smaller tribes consist of the **self-taught data scientist**, **the software platform user**, and **the domain specialist**.
It's also important to note here that data scientists and data engineers are now considered to be completely different things, even if in the early days the two roles were frequently mixed up and even if data scientists usually have a computer science background but also have some data engineering skills.

The Major Tribes
So, let's take a quick look at the tree major tribes, namely, computer scientists, statisticians, and other quantitative specialists.

Computer Scientists
Computer scientists are the people who have degrees in computer science and then did a master's or PhD in machine learning. The advantages are that they usually have very good skills in coding, databases, and software, but the issue is that they usually ignore traditional statistical techniques in theory, which can be useful in some particular domains and problems.

Computer scientists are very good for issues in machine learning tasks such as predictive modeling. Quite often they'll have experience in Kaggle competitions, which is a prime example of this kind of problem.

Note that Kaggle is a platform that runs predictive modeling and analytics competitions. Companies and users upload datasets and then statisticians, data scientists, and/or other specialists compete to create the best possible models for predicting and describing those datasets. It's a form of crowd sourcing and relies on the idea that countless strategies can be employed in a predictive modeling task and one can't know ahead of time which analyst or approach will be the best. Kaggle is now part of Google Cloud.
You're given a dataset and you just want to find a good algorithm to predict something. The fact that most computer scientists have solid coding skills means it's easier to integrate their work with the rest of the platform, especially if you're a small company or a startup. The majority will be using Python and won't have any problem writing their own APIs. So, essentially, you can use their skills to do many things at once, as they can write the code and integrate it as well.

Also, they have solid database skills, so they can do a lot of data engineering work. If you have your own data engineers, it's still worth it because it's easy for these people to retrieve the data, wrangle it into something usable, and so on.

This will save your developers time. They might also be able to make suggestions pertaining to the structure of the database, making your life even easier.

However, they have a lack of proper knowledge of statistics so for some particular problems where statistics is appropriate, such as research design, these people can't really help you.

Statisticians

Statisticians are people who usually have a degree in statistics. They might even have a master's or PhD, which can be in statistics or machine learning. They generally have a good theoretical grounding in the field, but they don't have the coding or database skills.

Statisticians have very solid knowledge of statistics and theory. They are the best people if what you are interested in is research design or statistical modeling because you want to know the driving factors behind something. They're also the best option if you want to model advanced complicated problems while at the same time making sure that the modeling process is transparent, and you understand what's happening.

They are also excellent at taking a critical look at the work of other data scientists because of the rigorous training in math and theory. The problem is, though, that most of the time they don't really have very good skills in coding and databases. The most likely language they'll be using is R, which they will use as a tool. They probably don't have any experience in other languages

or in databases, which will make it more difficult and time consuming to integrate their work within the system.

Also, some statisticians don't have much training in predictive modeling. On its own, predictive modeling is rarely considered to be important in the context of statistics and is more aligned with machine learning.

So, check if they have any Kaggle experience. It also pays to ensure that they're familiar with some sort of machine learning notions, such as cross validation, if you're interested in using their skills for predictive modeling.

Other Quantitative Specialists

Finally, we have what I call other quantitative specialists. These are people who come from disciplines heavy in math, such as physics, mathematics, actuarial science, econometrics, and so on. These people might have a master's degree or PhD degree, but this won't be in machine learning or statistics.

These are basically people who figured out that there are more (and better jobs) in data science than in their field of study, and they are trying to change careers. They are trying to capitalize their knowledge in math and/or coding in order to make that happen. You will see a huge variation in terms of skills and knowledge in this tribe.

These quantitative specialists are a bit special because they often have some solid skills and bring a diversity of thinking that's very important in data science. Furthermore, if the problem you're dealing with is in their specific domain, they are definitely amazing people to hire.

However, the problem is that they often lack rigorous training in machine learning or statistics, which can pose a serious problem in certain situations. So, when it comes to other quantitative specialists, it tends to be subjective in the sense that it depends on the person. However, the main drawback is that these people often lack formal education in the field.

They tend to be self-taught and you need to understand this fact and check to see how effective they are. You can likely find examples of their work on GitHub or Kaggle, for example. And you really want to check beforehand. Please note that being self-taught is not a bad thing—far from it. However, you need to check to ensure their skills are on par with your needs. These are often people who studied one field and discovered the pay isn't that brilliant or finding a job was virtually impossible. Then they discover being a data scientist comes with a hefty paycheck, so a chemist might decide, for example, to create a few mini projects, upload them to GitHub, or take part in a few competitions on Kaggle in an attempt to find a job as a data scientist.

In my experience, of all the specialties these people have, I've found that the people who are the most effective are physicists. Physics is full of applied math, which makes it easy for them to read machine learning papers, especially since it's, in essence, the same type of math. Furthermore, physicists need to be able to do a little coding themselves, so the skillset is similar to the one required in machine learning.

Something important to note is that domain specialists will have expertise in their respective fields, which might prove useful to you. For example, you might want to hire someone who has some experience in econometrics and a little bit of machine learning knowledge because your problem is related to econometrics in some way. Or, you might want to hire a physicist because you are working with sensor data or radar data.

However, you have to be careful with these other quantitative specialists because some of them will try to fake it. They'll go through a few tutorials and online courses for 2 weeks and, suddenly, they believe they're data scientists.

And that's just because they want to get the job. You have to be really cautious of these people because they can derail your whole project and cause a lot of problems.

This doesn't mean that you shouldn't consider people who have little experience but are honest about it and prove they are smart and willing to learn. They want to gain more experience and are intelligent people who have the potential to become outstanding data scientists. However, in my opinion, it's best to take these people on in a junior position with someone more experienced to oversee them. Of course, the person overseeing them should be a senior data scientist. If you don't have a senior data scientist, hire one first. Then, you can follow their progress as a junior and see how they grow. Depending on their evolution, you can choose to promote them or not.

Convergence Point

It's important to note that after about 5 or 6 years of experience, there's usually a convergence point in all the tribes. In other words, when someone has gained a lot of years of experience and has participated in quite a few projects—let's say between 10 and 30—and they've worked for different companies in various fields, they've usually picked up a wide range of skills. If they have a PhD, that's just an added bonus.

So, they'll have done some coding in both R and Python, and they'll have picked up a little of this, a little of that, and, pretty much, a little of everything. They also have a very good awareness of what's out there. This means that they know all the methods and techniques that are available, even if they don't know how to implement them themselves.

This is important because they know how a problem should be solved. And even if they don't know how to do it themselves, they'll know who to speak to and who to hire to get the work done. Sometimes, it's not important to have the skill per se, but to be aware of one's limitations and have the knowledge of what solutions are available and how to access the people who can implement them.

So, if you see someone who started out as a physicist but has been in data science for 10 years and has worked for a lot of companies in a wide range of fields, then this is the type of person who will likely fall in this category. Thus, when you find someone who has a lot of experience, you shouldn't worry too much about their background. What's more important is what they've learned over the years and whether they actually have the skills and the awareness of all the techniques and methods that are available.

What you do need to be careful about is when someone has a lot of experience, but they've worked on the same one or two projects for years and years. These are not the type of people I'm referring to.

I'm talking about people who have actively tried to learn new things over the years, such as gaining experience with R, with Python, maybe a little research design, and so on and so forth.

The Smaller Tribes

So, now let's take a look at the smaller tribes. When I say smaller tribes, I'm referring to the fact that there aren't as many people in these tribes as there are in the larger tribes. Also, these people tend not to really be data scientists but mainly people with some analytical skills. Thus, we have the self-taught people. These are usually people who studied something random or maybe even software development. They might have participated in a few Kaggle competitions and that's about the limit of their experience.

While the quantitative specialists from the larger tribes might also be self taught in certain respects, their discipline will have already taught them some skills which carry over to data science. In this particular situation, I'm referring to someone who studied humanities, for example. An art historian who suddenly discovers their field doesn't offer a lot of professional opportunities or an archaeologist who's discovered that digging through the dirt isn't quite as fun or financially rewarding as they had hoped, and then they suddenly decide to become a data scientist. Then we have the software platform user, which is someone who just knows how to use a specific tool, such as a dashboard, or a software like Weka8 (which you see in Figure 8-2) or RapidMiner.9 These people can offer real value for money if you only have a simple problem. For example, if all you need is some reporting, then these people are the best option because they'll definitely be cheaper.

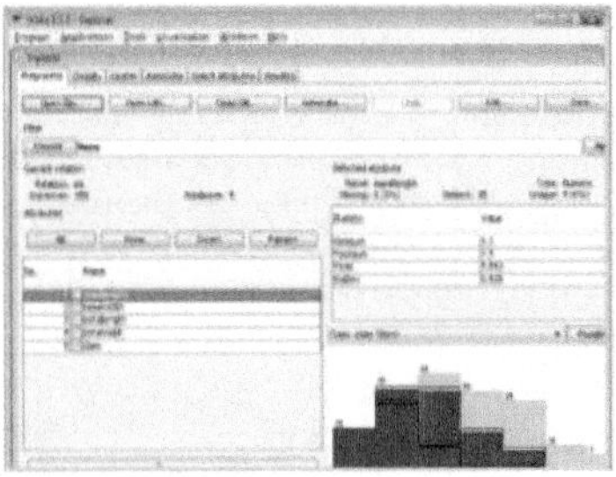

Figure 8-2. The Weka Explorer graphical user interface

They'll also be a lot happier with the work you give them compared to someone with a PhD in deep learning, for example. Otherwise, it would be like hiring a master chef to fry two eggs when as line cook can do just as good a job without being irritated by the work. However, someone like this won't be able to help you with more complicated problems because they might actually fall into the danger zone we discussed previously which is shown in the Venn diagram at the beginning of this chapter.

In other words, they lack a proper background in math and statistics, so they'll be able to apply the tool to certain situations, but they aren't the people you want to trust with building a model or predictive tool.

Last but certainly not least, we have the domain specialist. This is someone who has very advanced knowledge of machine learning but is limited to a very small niche. One of the most common examples is someone who is specialized in deep learning and computer vision. These are people who have done undergrad work in computer vision or have a master's or PhD in computer vision.

Now, if your problem is computer vision-related, then they are definitely the ones to hire because they will be amazing. But if you have a different issue, these aren't always the best people to turn to. Obviously, it won't be difficult for them to pick up new skills if they are doing machine learning or statistics on an advanced level. However, it might take them a few months to get up to speed with the knowledge required to solve different types of problems.

So, you have to be careful because if they fall into the danger zone, these domain specialists could cause more problems than you realize. It's really a good time to keep in mind the saying that if all you have is a hammer, then everything looks like a nail. For example, someone who is an expert in deep learning and has been doing it their whole life might believe that they can solve every problem using deep learning, which is not accurate. This is why you need to be careful. After all, sometimes you just need a fly swatter to get rid of that pesky buzzing.

However, as I previously mentioned, you should consider being more open to people who are aware of their limitations and are looking beyond their usual domains because they want to try something new. These people know it will take them a few months to learn the particulars of the new field, but they are more than willing to put the work in. Sometimes, taking this route pays off in more ways than one because you'll also earn their loyalty in the process as there aren't as many employers out there who are as enlightened as you and willing to give them a chance.

EXAMPLE: HOW TO EVALUATE A DATA SCIENTIST?

Whom would you rather hire to become your data scientist?
1. Someone who has finished in a top 10 university with an MSc in Machine Learning?
2. A developer who taught himself how to do data science?
3. Someone with a degree in statistics and 10+ years of experience?

The truth is that there is no correct answer. Job performance can depend on multiple factors. A quick search on Google Scholar returns a huge number of results. For example, the search term "IQ and job performance" returns more than 200,000 studies, most of them citing a correlation between IQ and job performance of around 0.5, which is significant. The term "years of experience and job performance" returns more than 4 million results, and the term "job performance predictors" returns more than 1 million results, with papers citing factors from emotional intelligence to personality.

The truth is that it in every case is different. In data science and technology, it is easy to find cases of employees with great credentials, who fail to perform on their role. Cultural fit, personality factors, and personal circumstances can all play a role in an employee's performance.

However, what you can do in order to make sure that employees perform at their best is to create the right environment. This is why in the appendix you are going to find some tools that can help you structure a data science project in a way that you can define clear outcomes and understand what skills someone should have to help you out with this project.

As a rule of thumb, when you are hiring for projects that are non-time critical, then cognitive abilities, IQ, and drive might be the most important factors.10 If, for example, you have a data science team in place that can help nurture someone with the right drive, then you might be able to get someone on a not very high salary, who will grow alongside the rest of your data science team.

On the other hand, when you are under time constraints, the best approach is to hire someone with the lots of experience and credentials. If the challenge you are facing is very well-defined, then hiring someone who has solved this exact challenge in the past can be a great idea.

Building A Data Science Culture

CHAPTER 9

Building A Data Science Culture

So, as I promised earlier, we are now going to look at the data science culture. We're going to see what a data science culture looks like and what you need to do to start building one in your own company.

An Overview of the Data Science Culture

First, let's take a look at what it means to have a data science culture.

Understanding What a Data Science Culture Is About

Before I get into the actual topic, I'd like to talk a little about the movie Moneyball. If you haven't seen this film yet, I urge you to do so because it is relevant to the situation at hand. In other words, it's all about building a datacentric culture within an organization.

The film is based on the book with the same name and, basically, describes Billy Beane's work at Oakland Athletics. This baseball team was pretty much one of the worst teams in the American baseball championship. However, thanks to Billy Beane's efforts, the team basically goes from the bottom of the pile to being one of the best teams and actually a lead contender.

Beane did this by using analytics and statistics. Essentially, he analyzed players, and even though their individual performance was poor, he saw that together they would make a great team. So, he acquired them, and because of their poor individual performance, other teams thought they were losers and they were cheap to acquire. So, basically, he put together an amazingly good team on a budget.

Throughout the team, you see the resistance Brad Pitt—who plays the role of Billy Beane—encounters because of the traditional ways of thinking practiced by veterans in the club. They simply will not accept the new approach he's trying to implement. Of course, he proves them wrong.

It's a very interesting movie , but I won't talk about it further. You should definitely watch it if you are interested in the topic, which I'm assuming you are since you are reading this book.

Now, let's break down the importance of a data science culture.

The Three Levels of a Data Science Culture

A data science culture should be analyzed on three levels, namely, the management level, the employee level, and the organizational level (Figure 9-1).

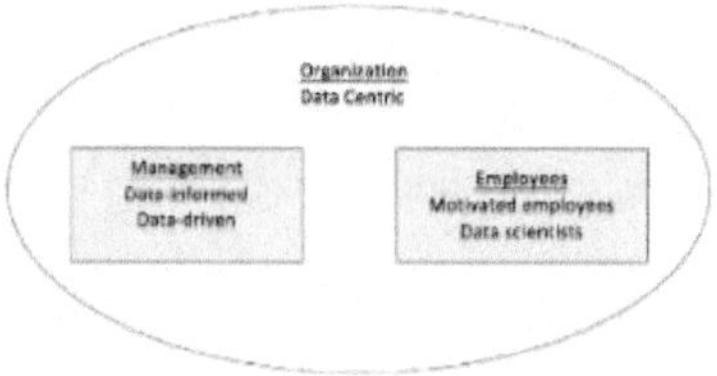

Figure 9-1. A data-centric organization encapsulates data-driven management, a data-friendly workforce, and data scientists

The Management Level

At the management level, it's all about being rational vs. being driven by your gut or taking a traditional approach, like in Moneyball. At this level, in a data science culture, the only role guts play is for food digestion, which is what they're there for in the first place.

It's also about being data informed and data driven. We'll look a little closer at these terms in a moment.

The Employee Level

On an employee level, it's all about what we previously discussed, namely, about hiring data scientists and managing them. It's about finding the right people and creating a friendly environment for them. It is also about making sure that the staff that needs to interact with the data scientists (software developers, product managers, etc.) are data aware and believe in the use of data science.

The Organizational Level

On an organizational level, having the right culture means combining the right elements from the management level and the employee level. The result is a data-centric organization. This will enable you to maximize the impact of data science from the data collection phase to the research and application phases. That's when you'll start seeing some real results within your organization.

Being Data Informed and Data Driven

Let's start off by looking at the difference between being data informed and data driven. When we say that an organization or a person is data informed, it means that they are actually using data and the context of data as inputs into their conversation and decision-making process. So, if you're using things such as dashboards and KPIs, for example, then you are data informed. Nowadays, it's very easy to be data informed. You can use Excel or another simple tool and it's not that difficult to make a few simple charts to see what's happening within your organization. Being data driven means taking it to the next level. This is when you start using more intelligent algorithms and methods to get the data. Then you transform the decision-making process by using the algorithm to make the decision for you or by taking the algorithm's output into account. What's the opposite of this approach? Well, the opposite of being data informed or data driven is when you use your guts to make a decision. Or tradition, which isn't much better in terms of accuracy or effectiveness.

Let's take a look at a few more examples.
When you are data informed, you might be using a dashboard or Excel to collect data from multiple sources. You've, of course, organized the data appropriately as we've previously discussed in Chapter 2 and have made sure to document the process to avoid any issues. The data is also accessible, and all your employees know about it and are aware of where it can be located and how they can use it. Being data driven means taking things a step further. This is where most companies should strive to be in the future. When you get to this point, it means that you are allowing the data and data science to help you make potentially disruptive decisions. In some cases, they might even completely replace human decision-making. So, if you trade using algorithms, for example, then you are data driven. If your app or website uses a recommender system, then you are data driven.

Obviously, being data driven does not mean that an algorithm needs to make every decision, but it does mean that you use algorithmic outputs in some parts of the organization and in the decision-making process. So, why would you want to do this? Being data driven improves efficiency and can actually improve decision-making. For example, a recommender system can make better decisions than humans as to what the client might want. Also, if you want to sell at a massive scale, after a certain point you need to have an algorithm that can actually replace humans when recommending items or curating content. This is just one example but there are many others in different industries.

WARNING

So, why would you want to do this? Being data driven improves efficiency and can actually improve decision-making. For example, a recommender system can make better decisions than humans as to what the client might want. Also, if you want to sell at a massive scale, after a certain point you need to have an algorithm that can actually replace humans when recommending items or curating content. This is just one example but there are many others in different industries.

Eric Peterson calls out a discussion on "What the C-suite should know about analytics" from Kishore Swaminathan, Accenture's chief scientist2:

Data is a double-edged sword. When properly used, it can lead to sound and well-informed decisions. When improperly used, the same data can lead not only to poor decisions but to poor decisions made with high confidence that, in turn, could lead to actions that could be erroneous and expensive.

In other words, if you use data and data science right, you'll see improved efficiency and better margins. However, if you don't use data in the right way, then it's very easy to end up in the danger zone in Figure 9-2, repeated from the previous chapter.

The problem is that you end up in a position where you use data in the decision-making process, and because you don't have the right theory, or you didn't run the right tests, the decisions are wrong. However, you're still fully confident because you think you used a scientific approach.

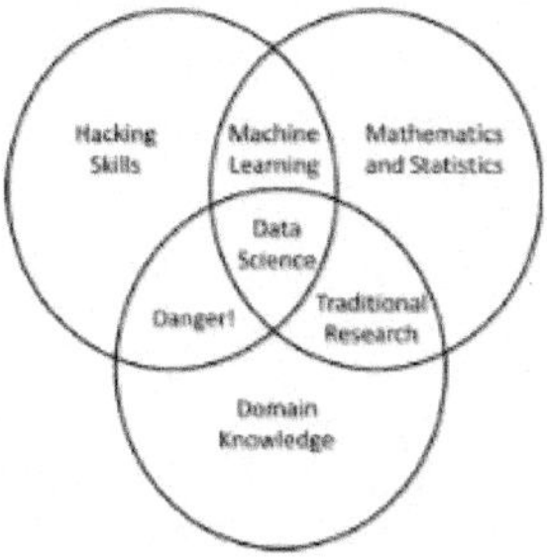

Figure 9-2. The data scientist Venn diagram

The easiest way to mitigate this risk is to hire data scientists who cover the mathematics and statistics circle in the diagram and will use the right theory and processes to do data science. Of course, you need the right culture so that the scientists can interact with other divisions and everyone can scrutinize everyone else's work.

Creating a Friendly Environment for Data Scientists

At the employee level, you want to create a friendly environment for data scientists. We've already covered a lot of this in the previous chapter on hiring data scientists. In essence, you need to remember that data scientists are not only after monetary rewards. They also want the right culture, they want to be mentally stimulated, they want to feel that they are making progress, that they are learning new things, and that their work has an impact. Also, keep in mind that data scientists tend to be introverts. It's important for everyone to work in teams with people they like and the right culture, but for these people it can be even more important than the average person.

Keeping all this in mind is the key to having happy employees, which translates into increased productivity.

Building A Data Science Culture

Being Data-Centric on an Organizational Level
An organization is data-centric when data science is at the core, which means a few different things.

First of all, it means that you have a 360-degree view of what is happening in terms of data and data science. Data science is a separate division, meaning the data scientist has more freedom and the license to explore new things, even if they are potentially disruptive. They have more responsibility, which can motivate them more but also carry a greater degree of risk. However, because you have this 360-degree view, you can mitigate this risk. The right communication and reporting channels exist between all important divisions, especially between the developers and the data scientist, but also between the data scientist and the management.

This is important because you want to make sure that the work the data scientist does has an impact and also because you need to be aware of the data that's being collected, how it gets used, and how it's all implemented, which is very easy to get lost in.

To clarify, when we talk data collection, there are two large issues decision makers need to be aware of. One is legal issues, which have become very important nowadays because of the GDPR in the EU and the United Kingdom. There are all kinds of issues with data privacy, and there's really no excuse not to be aware of how data is being used and how it's collected.

Secondly, it's important to be aware of what the data scientist is researching and also to make sure it's implemented and used in the organization in a positive way. So, this is where having effective communication channels becomes very important. One department can scrutinize the work of another to make sure that what's being done is relevant to the organization.

Let's look at a few examples of how things can go wrong.

Example 1: When Data Is Not at the Core
Let's start with an example of what happens when data science is not at the core. This tends to happen in small or medium enterprises that are trying to reduce costs because they're short on cash.

When a company wants to do data science, but they don't want to hire a new person, they might turn to their own personnel to do data science. They might hire a developer to do machine learning, but that's about it.

It's not a bad idea as someone supervises the software developer. Otherwise, someone might run a model that they got from a library , and they don't know how to properly test this model.

They might use a cross-validation scheme, for example. The model goes into production , and you end up with disastrous results because you're in the danger zone. In other words, you're using a person who has the hacking skills and the domain expertise, but they don't have the theoretical knowledge to back it up.

So, you make decisions that you're very confident in, but they're actually wrong. Technically, it's worse to be wrong and be confident in your mistakes than it is to just be wrong.

Example 2: Things Don't Get Implemented

Another common example that happens mainly in big organizations where there are personnel issues and communication problems is when you hire data scientists and things do not get implemented.

While there are a few ways things might not get implemented, let's look at the case of a data scientist who is not familiar with a domain. So, you hire someone who looks really good on paper. You also really believe in data science, and you give them the freedom and the resources to do whatever they want.

The problem is that it's very easy to create silos in these cases, especially when data scientists speak another language in a sense to other departments. A common mistake is that a data scientist spends months working on some- thing and then it can't be implemented because they were not familiar with the domain. They couldn't understand that what they were creating couldn't be implemented because of real work constraints or due to lack of relevancy from a business perspective. This tends to happen a lot with people who recently finished their PhDs, and they're still in this very academic mindset of trying to do complicated and fancy things instead of simple things that have an impact. Thus, having the right culture in data science is not just about being data informed but about transforming creativity into results. It's about giving the data scientist freedom and resources but also making sure the proper checks are in place to ensure the work is relevant and can and will be implemented.

Example 3: Poor Communication

Another example of when things can go wrong is when you have poor communication, which happens quite frequently.

Let's say that there's no one to oversee the communication between the soft- ware developer and the data scientist. Even though they are both technical people, they speak a different language most of the time. The result is the creation of silos, which are then difficult to break down. And silos lead to bad practices and increase development times.

First, the problem is the different styles of communication. For example, does the data scientist like to speak a lot using math and different expressions compared to the developers? Also, lack of knowledge of each other's prac- tices is an issue.

Developers like things to be well documented and they like to run tests. Data scientists, on the other hand, can have different approaches. They might even use different programming languages, which can also be an issue.

A solution, in this case, would be to try to make people work in pairs. Another option would be to hire people who have machine language experience, and they can compensate for the poor communication between the data scientist and the developer.

Or you might want to do the opposite and hire a data scientist with some software development experience.

Others have proposed trying to enforce particular software development methodologies across all departments.

The problem is that these don't always work mainly because data science is a bit different to software development and sometimes you can find yourself in an awkward situation. So, the main difference is that progress in data science is not incremental as it usually is in software development. It's a bit more all or nothing.

You might spend a few weeks doing research and then you suddenly get results. Conversely, in software development you might add a new feature every day.
So, even if it's not a bad idea to have stand-ups, for example, where people can share what they're working on every day, don't take into account all the suggestions for software methodologies. You can, of course, think about them, but then adapt them to your specific situation.

MONEYBALL: A STORY ABOUT DATA SCIENCE CULTURE
The world of sports used to be very detached from the world of technology and statistics. Most sports professionals would probably find a discussion about databases or machine learning algorithms pretty boring. Sports was an entirely different world, and Billy Beane's approach seemed alien to the baseball establishment.

Billy Beane had the insight that most of the metrics that were being used in the game were outdated. Players were chosen by scouts who used to be coaches or players themselves. Billy Beane figured out that statistics like the on-base percentage (how often a batter reaches base) were better predictors of success than other statistics that had been traditionally used.

This way, Oakland A's were able to create completely different valuations than the ones that had been used in the past and compete with a budget of around $44 million with teams that were spending nearly three times as much. This approach was called "sabermetrics." The term is derived from the acronym SABR, which stands for Society for American Baseball Research.

Unfortunately, Oakland A's didn't manage to win the championship (even if they got very close to winning it), and then they lost their advantage, once other clubs started copying their approach. Since then the world of sports has been invaded by data science, with devices and algorithms ruling many aspects of the game. There are conferences in sports analytics being held, with the biggest taking place in MIT's Sloan School of Management
(www. sloansportsconference.com).

Steps to Build a Data Science Culture Let's take a look at the steps you need to take to build a culture that is conducive to data science.
Why Do You Need Data Science in the First Place?

First, you need to ask yourself why you need data science. There are three common scenarios in businesses:

1. Data science is an integral part of your business: maybe you're an AI or robotics company, or you're in deep tech in some way, in which case you usually have to have the knowledge yourself.

2. You run a company and want to improve efficiency, so maybe you want to improve operations, for example.

3. You want to improve sales so maybe you want to build your recommender system to improve your B2C offer.

It's unlikely that you fall into the first category or you wouldn't be reading this book. So, you're in either in two or three, and obviously these can be combined.
At this point, you need to ask yourself why you need data science, so you know where you're going next. Now, let's look at resistance to change.

Resistance to Change
If you're a startup, then you're most likely flexible so resistance to change won't be an issue. If you are part of a big organization, though, the following will be very relevant.
The three types of resistance to change are cultural, personal, and intellectual (Figure 9-3).

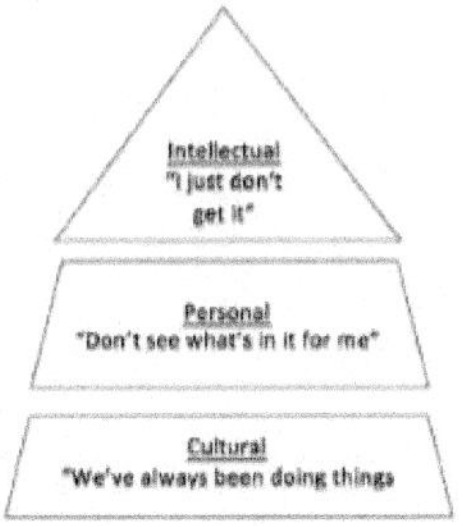

Figure 9-3. Types of resistance to change

Cultural Resistance to Change

Cultural resistance to change is what we see in Moneyball. We have a big and old organization or multiple layers of management or fields that haven't had much to do with math, statistics, or data. A good example is the comparison between sports and finance.

As shown in Moneyball, the world of sports is still trying to get deeper into analytics, but it's just not there yet. Even back when the events of Moneyball took place, the kind of things that Billy Beane tried to implement in Oakland Athletics are nothing special in finance, which is usually one of the fields at the forefront of data analysis.

Personal Resistance to Change

Personal resistance to change also occurs in smaller companies and is when employees don't like the change. To give you an example from personal experience, I worked with a client and waited 2 months for someone to give me a database expert. Then, I had to call the supervisor and wait another month. What may have happened is that the employees could have been over-worked and they were handed even more work. So, the employees don't really see any benefit out of doing anything, like exporting a database or trying to implement an algorithm.

Intellectual Resistance to Change

Finally, we have the case where people are afraid of what they don't understand. Think Skynet in The Terminator movie, as in when people are terrified that machines will take over the world.

There isn't a lot of intellectual resistance to change in organizations because most understand that data can be useful since it can improve efficiency and sales. However, if there's the slightest hint of intellectual resistance to change, this is where hiring a good data officer can be a good start. This is someone who can own the data and can show it to people, as well as showing how it can improve pretty much everything within a company.

Building A Data Science Culture

The Journey to Change

When it comes to your journey to change, there are three important points to remember. First, you have to determine how data scientists will get you there. This means creating a data science-friendly environment where they can talk about it and trying to run projects with a large potential impact. Change is slow, but if people start seeing results, then they'll slowly change their minds because they will understand the benefits.

It's very important to also find a champion in some cases. This is someone who can create enthusiasm in this new direction. The champion is someone who truly believes in this new approach, and they have the enthusiasm and the status to actually push the rest of the company toward this new goal.

It's usually a high-ranking employee who is also well liked. It could be you or it could be a data scientist or the chief data officer.

Generally, the best option is for it to be someone who is already in the organization and is popular, someone people respect and listen to regardless of what they're talking about. This could also help employees see this as a learning experience and something more positive for the company and hence for themselves.

The final point to remember on your journey to change is that it's important to focus on benefits for the employees because everyone hates having to do more work with no reward. However, employees who are intellectually curious and driven will see the benefits of learning and also helping the organization since this can translate into results for themselves.

How to Start

When it comes to implementing a data science culture, I've seen two approaches. The first is the baby steps approach, and the second is the use case approach.

In the baby steps approach, you collect lots of data and the decision makers educate themselves in data science. Then, they try to use simple graphs and stats, so they become more data informed. Once they feel comfortable with the data, they take the next step and hire someone to make sense of the data.

The use case approach is more of a top-down approach. This is when a company has a certain type of problem, and they set up a plan and might start by hiring someone to help them design the plan and solve the particular problem. Then, they'll consider how the findings are relevant to other use cases.

The baby steps approach is the most common because it's easy to collect and visualize data in Excel or maybe a

dashboard. This happens when a company is interested in data because they hear that everyone else is collecting and using data, but it's not really a priority.

So, at one point the company has solved its main problems and is profitable, and they decide to hire someone because they have all this data and want to do something with it. This approach makes sense because it's not too disruptive to current operations, and if data collection is not your priority, you don't have to push things too far, too fast.

However, it can also cause all sorts of problems. It's a slower way of adopting data science, but then you also get all the issues we talked about in Chapter 2. In other words, a bunch of data is collected with no prior thought or goal, and it turns into a disaster.

The use case approach is less common, and it happens when the company has a clear use case. The advantage is that it can provide more immediate results using a more targeted approach. However, it requires some level of data awareness and the company needs to have access to a data scientist they can trust.
Note that a company doesn't have to choose one approach over another. Quite often they might start with the first approach and end up with the latter.

Where to Start
The where is just as important as the how. So, you first want to map your organization's use of data. You need to understand the flow of data from collection to usage and discover any dark data you might have.

Also, emphasize strategy and innovation and try to help employees understand why this is important. Reward good behavior, which is very important for data scientists. Many data scientists want recognition and to feel as if they are making an impact on the world or in their company. Thus, promoting good work on a blog and social media will help a lot, as well as sharing the best use cases with everyone in the company.

Finally, creating an embedded culture is the way to break down silos and improve communication. You want data scientists to work closely with developers, the product owners, and the managers. This is the only way to make sure that the research is relevant, that the results are implemented, and that they have an impact within the company.

Understanding and Using Dark Data
Dark data is operational data that is not being used, such as log files, notes from sales calls or emails, and similar information.

This type of data is relevant because there's a lot of it an, and it's sitting there gathering dust. Deloitte reports that by 2020 we're going to have 44ZB of data.3 This figure might not be 100% accurate, but it's still a huge amount of data. Note that many of the sources of data aren't specified; it includes audio, notes, video, image files, and so on.

Also, Deloitte has a special mention for the Internet of Things and other non-traditional sources. This type of data is easy to collect, but it's not always used. So, it very quickly becomes dark data and just sits in a data warehouse waiting for someone to make sense of it.

What Can Dark Data Do for You?
There are a number of things dark data can do for you, but it's not easy to provide a general set of guidelines that will apply in every situation. However, here are a few examples.

So, you might have some email address. In some cases, you can extract gender and age from email addresses or visitor behavior from log files or sentiment from customer calls. Then, you can create predictive models for user retention from the usage logs or customer logs, for example. This is just one example and there are countless possibilities.

Keep in mind that the unstructured nature of data can make it difficult to use. However, if you can do it, it can be very rewarding.

Other Steps to Take to Become More

Data Driven
As mentioned, you need to create an open culture that promotes strategy and innovation. A champion can be a vital asset as they help motivate employees.
There are a number of ways you can create this kind of culture. You can, for example, organize internal hackathons once or twice a month or allow employees to play around with an idea of their own. Other companies have done this successfully, and it works because it keeps people happy and engaged.

Another interesting approach is to use Kaggle to create internal competitions. This works if you have a very large number of data scientists within your company. It gives people an opportunity to have some fun and learn something new.

Finally, if you can, open up your data and allow your employees to invite other people to take part in small projects. Of course, this doesn't apply for every company. However, if you can, it can be a great way to find new talent.

Rewarding Good Behavior

When it comes to rewarding good behavior, employees with good ideas need some form of recognition. Maybe you publish their results on a blog, or you make libraries and software open source and attribute the developers. This is what large organizations in the field are doing.

For example, Google and Facebook have their own research blogs. Facebook also has a forecasting library called Prophet when you can read an article written by the people within the company who created the library.

This is an excellent approach because everyone wants to be rewarded for their contribution to something new and amazing. And there's no reason for them to be anonymous. Their names are right there. Plus, data scientists like to look into the future. If they want to get another job, it's good for them to know that a new employer can easily find them and their work online. This is why data scientists and software developers also have GitHub accounts.

So, it's not just about the bonuses, it can also be about the ego.

Create an Embedded Culture

Finally, one of the most important things to do when trying to build the right culture for data science is to create an embedded culture. This means that you want the data scientist to work closely with other divisions, and you want to have good communication between all parties, as well as full transparency.

Stand-ups where people share what they are working on are a pretty standard way of promoting communication and transparency. However, be careful because daily stand-ups can get irritating because of the slow nature of a data scientist's work. It isn't incremental and the last thing you want is to have a bunch of introverts feeling uncomfortable because they have no results to show. This is why weekly stand-ups might be a better option.

You also should consider mentorship programs for new data scientists. Junior data scientists can be very enthusiastic, and sometimes you can find amazing talent from some good universities who might be a bit inexperienced. This might be their first real job, so it's a good idea to have a senior data scientist educate them and mentor them, which will allow them to become great.

CASE STUDY: BOOKING.COM DOES DATA SCIENCE THE RIGHT WAY

Booking.com is a company that does data science right. They sell over 1.5 million hotel rooms every 24 hours, and millions of people browse the site constantly, which means they have massive amounts of data. They are continuously using that data to improve their services and develop new ones.

Booking.com has over 120 data scientists with different profiles, backgrounds, and working preferences. The culture is clearly data driven and has been developed in such a way that the company offers the perfect venue for data scientists. From challenging them with different projects that require them to constantly learn new things to helping with their education through workshops and presentations held by their peers, there is little opportunity for a data scientist to get bored at Booking.com.7

The structure is also one you want to emulate as it's embedded, like we previously discussed. Their data scientists are an integral part of the business. They are part of teams that include developers, product owners, and various other specialists. The team is formed in such a way that they can take an idea from concept to the implementation stage.

On a daily basis, they follow what they call the booking agile essentials recipe, which means they have daily stand-ups, backlog, retrospectives, KPIs and objectives and key results, team purpose, and more. This approach allows their teams to move forward or to fail and learn from their failure as quickly as possible.

For this reason, data scientists at Booking.com are expected to have excellent communication skills as well as commercial awareness. In other words, technical skills aren't enough.

However, data scientists are happy at Booking.com because they are constantly working on new projects and learning new things. They don't have to wait around for data to show up, their advice and recommendations are taken into account, they are allowed to take new approaches, and they are treated like the data scientists they are.

So, you could do worse than to emulate the Booking.com model in terms of creating a data-centric culture. Of course, you don't have to do everything they do. It is a huge company after all. Maybe, in your case, you don't care so much about communication, but are more interested in the technical aspect.

However, if you want to create an embedded culture, then definitely look into how Booking.com is doing it.

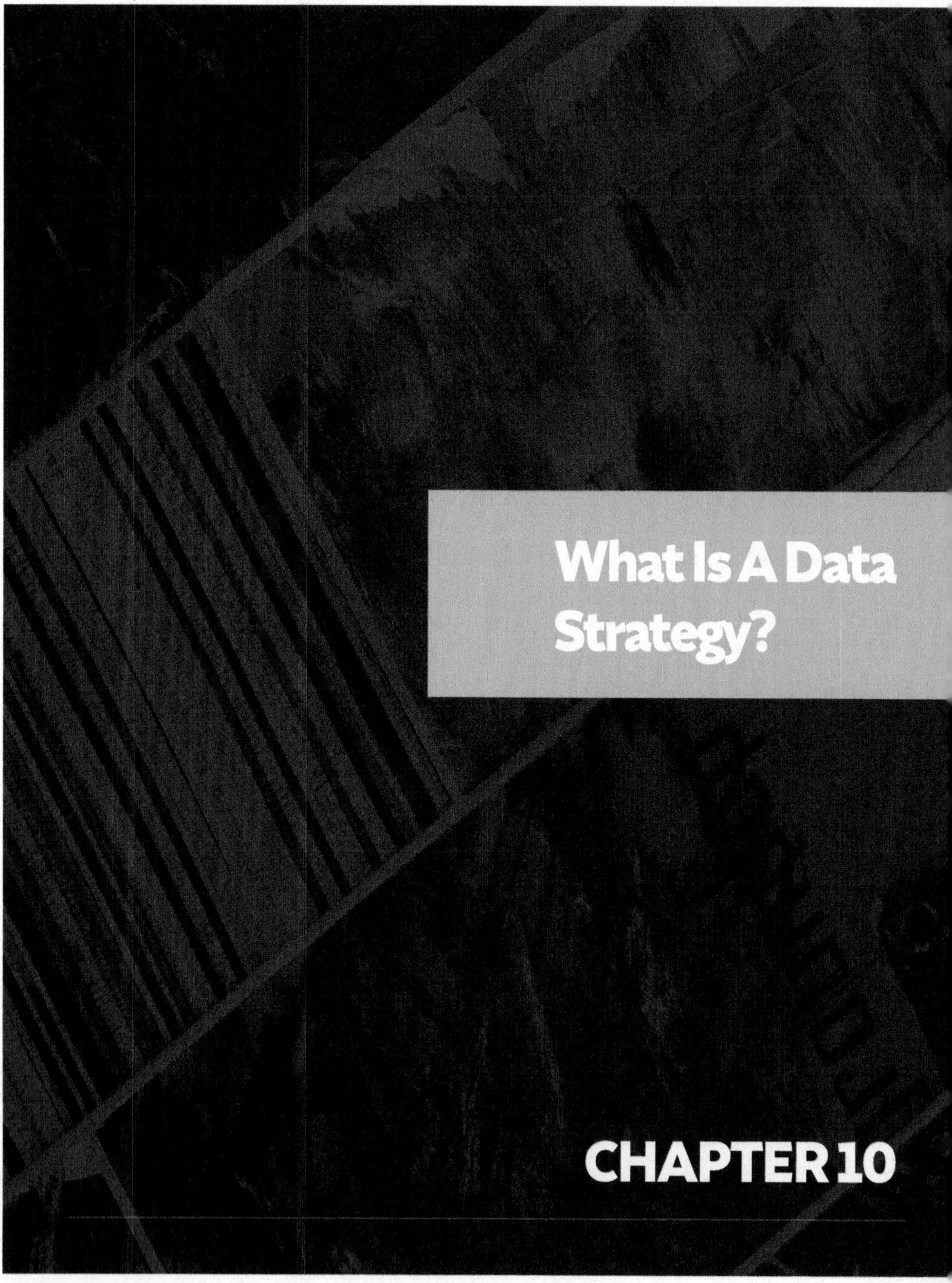

CHAPTER 10

What Is A Data Strategy?

What Is A Data Strategy?

Now that we have covered a high-level overview of data science, we move on to talk about data strategy. This is key for any business that wants to generate value from its data, and it is just as important as hiring the right person.
There are many varying definitions of a data strategy on the Internet, but a good definition would be the following:
A data strategy is a living document that defines how the business is setting itself up, both from a technical and organizational perspective, to proactively manage and leverage data toward the long-term business strategy.

This definition is made up of several key components:
A data strategy is a living document ... —A data strategy should not be a document that takes months to develop and then is put to one side, gathering dust for no one to read again. By all means, the data strategy can be a document, a presentation, or whatever other media you choose, but above all, it should be a living document—meaning that it is constantly updated and refreshed as the business evolves.

...defines how the business is setting itself up, both from a technical and organizational perspective...
—A good data strategy should ideally cover both the engineering and infrastructure approach and how you plan to structure the organization and teams to make the most of your data. ... to proactively manage and leverage data ...
—By creating a data strategy, you make sure that you take proactive measures to make the business as resilient as possible and give it as much of a competitive advantage as early as possible. ... toward the long-term business strategy—Last but certainly not least, a data strategy should not exist in isolation from the rest of the business. Instead, a good data strategy will have the business strategy as its north star, and all the plans should stem from this.

Why Is a Data Strategy Important?
Have you ever wondered what happens every minute on the Internet? Google processes 3.8 million search queries, 4.5 million videos are watched on YouTube, 188 million e-mails are sent, and approximately 700,000 hours are watched on Netflix. As our lives have become increasingly digital, the interactions we have with products and services can be recorded and observed like never before.

What do Nike, L'Oreal, Vodafone, and Transport for London have in common? On the face of it, all of these businesses operate in different markets and offer completely different products.

However, they are all data-driven businesses.
In recent decades, data has transformed from being a side effect of products to one of the most

valuable assets in a business. Data is multifaceted in the way it can add value. Still, one can broadly categorize the areas where data adds value as operational improvements, customer insights, and data as a product.

1. Operational Improvements:

· Data can improve or even fully automate processes within our businesses. For example, Verizon uses data to triage customer service calls and thus optimize its call centers. In addition, data-rich business areas such as supply chain logistics are prime targets to be automated.

· Another example of this is how Netflix has invested large sums into optimizing the production process so they can create original content at scale (Kumar, Misra, Walraven, Sharan, Azarnoush, Chen, and Govind 2018).

2. Customer Insights:

· Many of today's most popular services use data as a tool to deliver a better product experience for the customer. For example, LinkedIn uses your past interactions to recommend posts you may be interested in. Spotify's Discover Weekly is another fantastic example of using data and ML to generate recommendations and increase user engagement.

3. Data as a Product:

· Finally, data in and of itself can add immense value to the business as a new revenue stream.

Typically, this area of value will only be relevant once a company has scaled to thousands of users and is generating significant amounts of data, but it should not be underestimated.

· Owning large amounts of user data can greatly increase the value of a company in the eyes of an acquirer. IBM acquired Weather Underground as part of a deal that was valued at approximately $2 billion by The Wall Street Journal, demonstrating the value of the data it possessed to IBM. While IBM didn't disclose how the data would be used, it is clear that there are integrations of weather data within many other aspects of the business (e.g., IoT) since weather data can affect device failure. Sometimes, even data that does not seem valuable can hide a wealth of information.

Keep these areas in mind as we explore how to build a good data strategy, as they will help guide your thinking. Even the European Union has acknowledged the importance of data in the future, outlining their own data strategy. The goal is to create a single data marketplace to level the playing field in competing against the big tech companies that own vast amounts of valuable data ("European Data Strategy" n.d.). Now that you are convinced that every business is a data business, it becomes clearer that a company needs an effective strategy to extract as much value as possible from the data it collects.

What Is A Data Strategy?

Oftentimes, especially at the earliest stages of a business, data collection can be expensive in terms of time and money. A well-thought-out data strategy helps to zoom in on which data will unlock the most value and hopefully kick off the data flywheel. Throughout my work, I have often seen these two types of situations, as shown in Table 10.1. So, what do these two cases have in common? In both cases, a data strategy can save the day. In the first case, a data strategy would have

Table 10.1 Data strategy situations

	Situation 1	Situation 2
Use Case	A company wants to conduct a statistical analysis. As the problem is investigated, it becomes clear that data could have been collected to improve the analysis, but it is not available.	A start-up requires some sort of data science service. As the discussion about the system progresses, it becomes clear that the requested service depends on many different kinds of data. The collection and storage of this data exposes new avenues for monetization that can help improve the start-up's revenue strategy.
Explanation	This is an example of what I like to call data debt, where the lack of planning for future projects has led to the company not collecting all the necessary data. As we will see in the following, a good data strategy will describe the projects a company wishes to aim for in the coming 12–24 months, along with the data required to deliver good results on those projects. Having a data scientist as part of the planning process will help make sure that you are covering your bases on all the data you should be collecting for the project.	In this particular situation, the impact of planning for a specific data science project is that more opportunities are discovered to leverage the data in the overall revenue strategy. Often, the brainstorming around a data strategy can go backward and forward. While thinking of the data required for one project, you may discover other projects and opportunities open up using that same data.
Example	A car rental company wants to forecast demand for the upcoming months to create customized deals for each client. The company is not keeping information regarding the marital status and the age of its users. This information could have been very easily collected on its platform throughout all these years of operation. However, since this was not done, the company has to settle for a suboptimal model with reduced performance.	A common case is a recommender system. A recommender system can benefit from all kinds of information about the users: age, gender, purchases, and possibly other things. Designing the platform to improve the information collected from its users results in an extensive and comprehensive database that can boost the recommender system's effectiveness and can also be used for other purposes. For example, this information could be used to better manage discount deals, improve advertising, or even enhance the user experience.

provided the company with tons of additional revenue. In the second case, a correctly implemented data strategy could provide the start-up with a competitive advantage in addition to increased revenues.

However, a data science strategy is less effective if it is not implemented from the early stages. This is why it is important to consider it as an integral plan of the product roadmap and the business plan. One of my favorite sayings is "failing to plan is planning to fail," which couldn't be more true for a data strategy.

How to Define a Data Strategy

Now that we've introduced the importance of having a data strategy, you must be wondering what the best process is to build a data strategy. There are many approaches that people favor online, each with its own pros and cons. The approach described as follows is one that we've had success with when working with small- to medium sized businesses looking to build a roadmap for working with data. Start With Your Business Strategy A data strategy cannot exist in isolation from a coherent business strategy. The type of work you undertake will largely depend on the objectives your business is looking to meet in the short- to medium term.

For example, imagine Company A (a B2C company) has just launched—or is about to launch—its first product to market. Presumably, one of their strategic priorities for the following year might be to rapidly acquire users and ensure that retention and engagement are high. Given these priorities, the data team must focus on building the right foundation to collect and analyze the necessary data to make rapid iterations on the product if necessary. In this example, this would form a core part of the data strategy.

Note that the business strategy will change from time to time, so it is important that the data strategy also adapts to meet any new objectives or priorities.

If you have a clear idea of your strategic priorities as a business, then feel free to skip to the section on data use cases. Otherwise, in the following section, we will describe an exercise that should help you focus on what is most important for the business right now.

Exercise 1: Defining Your Strategic Priorities

First, a company needs to identify why it exists—what we'll call its vision. This vision is the North Star for the company, and it should answer the question, "What will the world look like in 10 years with our company?" It should be bold, grand, and aspirational because, even if you never get there, it gives everyone in your company a sense of direction and purpose.

What Is A Data Strategy?

Following the vision statement, you should create your mission statement. This is a more short-term-focused description of why the organization does what it does, what it does, who it does it for, and how it does it. The mission statement should feel as if it's within your grasp and is something you are clearly working toward in the present.

Lastly, from the mission statement, one can derive their strategic priorities. The whole point of defining the vision and mission is that you should start seeing a path from the organization's current state to reach that North Star and this path is your strategy! All that's left is defining the strategy into concrete priorities. When going through this exercise with business owners in the past, we like to break down the business into its parts and get a feeling for where the areas for improvement are. The components we use to define a business are:

- Product
- Growth Marketing/Sales
- Internal Operations (People and processes)
- Business Model/Finance

These components will vary slightly depending on the type of business you're building, so change those as you see fit.

Once we've defined these components, the next step is to brainstorm some areas of work or improvement for each component (using a whiteboard tool or similar). It should come as no surprise that the more people that are involved from different parts of the business, the better the perspective you'll gain on each component. However, keep in mind that each additional person will make the brainstorming session longer, making it more difficult to dive deeper into each employee's opinions.

The output of this brainstorming exercise will be a set of ideas and suggestions for areas of work for the business going forward. You should begin to see certain themes emerging within each of the components or even across components. Take some time with the group to cluster all the thoughts and ideas into logical groups and decide which ones likely deserve the most attention in the coming year. These should form the foundation of your business strategy.

Build Your Data Use Cases From your strategic priorities, you can start to ideate what the data use cases could be to support the delivery of that strategy. A data use case is a well-contained and well-defined project that relates to completing one of your strategic objectives. The data use cases that you define will form your key priorities for the year ahead, and from these data use cases, you can begin to formulate a plan of your data activities.

Some examples of data use cases are:

- Build a self-serve analytics capability in the company;
- Reduce the cost of delivery of service for a particular product;
- Deliver a more personalized customer experience;
- Reduce customer churn.

A good number of data use cases would be 3 to 5 for a year, including 1 to 2 quick wins. A quick win data use case serves several purposes, namely that you can demonstrate near-immediate value from the data side of the business to get more buy-in from the rest of the business. Also, delivering a project end-to-end can help to uncover any unexpected issues before beginning work on any bigger projects.

Once you have identified your data use cases, you can start to break down what will be required to deliver each of them and what considerations to make before embarking on any of them. The areas you need to think about for each data use case are:

- **Data requirements:** Do you require any specific data to deliver the project? A data scientist will be able to guide you regarding the type of data that may be required for a project and the quantity.
- **Key project resources:** Think about the roles that will be required to deliver on your project—this could cover not only data engineers, data scientists, and data analysts but also any business owners, project/product managers, and so on. Also, think about which people in the business may be impacted by this project and need to be involved as stakeholders.
- **Technology:** Are there any technical dependencies before the project can be successfully implemented? Will the data architecture/infrastructure have to be modified to get all the required data?

It is useful to think of these areas for all data use cases together, so you can spot overlapping requirements across projects and better coordinate resources.

Data Architecture

Having a clear idea of how your data is architected is imperative for long-term success and continuous innovation. As your organization scales, the amount of data in your organization will scale, and often in a nonlinear manner since each new user could potentially be creating more data than previous users as your product grows and improves.

In the early stages of a company, the cost of switching from one database or architecture type to another is manageable. It can often be done without too much service downtime. Compare that with an organization like Slack, which spent three years (from 2017 to 2020) migrating their data architecture from active–active clusters to a tool called Vitess (Ganguli, Iaquinti, Zhou, and Chacon 2020). Clearly, the amount of due diligence, thought, and work put into this migration is eons above one that a start-up with fewer than a thousand users would have to make to move from NoSQL to a SQL database, for example.

The lesson here is that putting some careful consideration into your data and systems architecture early on can pay great dividends in the future. There are countless stories of organizations spending millions of dollars trying to fix data silos and merging data from countless sources to get a single version of the truth. Not to mention the potential sum in lost opportunities because of how difficult it was to quickly prototype and test new ideas.

The business case for putting some serious thought into the data architecture is irrefutable. However, in reality, there is a fine balancing act between spending endless hours designing the perfect architecture and implementing your best idea at the moment to move quickly.

If one follows the thinking of agile methodology, one can only make decisions under existing knowledge, and any assumption about what the future holds is just that, an assumption. Therefore, don't obsess over the perfect architecture, especially if there is still a lack of clarity around the product's future. Instead, it's more important to move quickly, test your assumptions, and keep iterating toward product-market fit.

Data Governance

Managing data across the organization is more than a technical or infrastructure challenge. It also relies heavily on the kind of governance a company puts in place to ensure that data is traceable, clearly defined, and accessible to only the people who need it. As with data architecture discussed previously, the scale of a data governance program should be proportional to the scale of data a business holds, meaning doesn't weigh down the business with too many processes early on.

A good place to start on data governance early is building a company-wide data dictionary. A data dictionary is a living document where all the raw and derived data that exists in an organization should be defined clearly. For any derived data, there should be an explanation of the original source of the data and any transformations applied to it. Building a data dictionary should highlight any areas of confusion or misunderstanding about the data and serve to align everyone in the company on where to search for data to create reports or metrics. It is also recommended to assign someone responsible for each data source. Those people can be contacted if any issues arise with the data or if people have questions or concerns.

Another crucial aspect of data governance is the processes required by law under regulations such as the General Data Protection Regulation (GDPR) or the California Consumer Privacy Act (CCPA). Again, a data dictionary will help massively in identifying what kind of personal data you hold about users, and you can record the answers to questions such as:

- Why is this personal data necessary?
- How long is this data archived after a user becomes inactive?
- What third-party software are we sharing this data with?

Managing an AI Project

The field of product management for software has been rising in popularity throughout the 20th and 21st centuries, as academics and entrepreneurs have been designing new approaches to manage the complexity of software projects. Most notably, this has led to the explosion of agile methodology, making it the go-to methodology for delivering products that users love.

While software development has had decades to learn and mature, AI product development is still in its infancy. As a result, AI product development presents new challenges not seen in software development: there are more unknowns, outcomes are nondeterministic, and there has been an influx of new tools, infrastructure, and processes to support AI development that people have to become familiar with.
However, perhaps most impactful is that AI shifts the concept of engineering from a deterministic process to a probabilistic one. With all these challenges in mind, one would think that the process to approach AI projects would need to differ from software. However, the reality is that most companies we've interacted with that are working on AI projects tend to shoehorn typical agile software methodologies to fit with these new kinds of projects.

In this section, we will explore in further detail why AI projects differ from software projects, and how product management practices should shift to deal with this shifting paradigm.

Why Are AI Projects Different to Software Projects?
As mentioned previously, the difference can be described at a high level by the fact that AI development is much more of a probabilistic process than a deterministic one. The following four areas describe in more detail how these projects differ and will help to clarify this concept some more:

Unpredictability. In traditional software projects, one can think of an overall project simplistically as a composition of functions where each function takes an input, and applies some heuristics and processing to that input. As a result, the function returns an output.
When all these small unit functions are put together, one can create all sorts of wonderful applications.

Since each function has been coded explicitly, it is simple enough to understand the behavior of each function by looking at what each line of code is doing. Doing so can help you understand not just typical test cases but also any edge cases that might cause the function to break. For example, if a function applies the logarithmic function to a set of inputs, any negative input will break it, so one can write some logic to reject any negative inputs.

If we continue this analogy in trying to explain the world of AI, one can think of AI as an approach to solving problems where we have pairs of input and output examples, and we're training a model to replicate the function that converts the inputs into the outputs. A simple case would be, if we had the pairs (1, 1), (2, 4), (3, 9), (7, 49), and (8, 64), then we would want our model to learn that the function is y = x2 .

In reality, the examples of input, and output pairs that we work with represent much more complicated functions than this, which makes ML such a valuable tool in the toolkit. Now, say we've built a model, and we wanted to understand the behavior of the resulting function like was explained in the software project. We can no longer examine each line of code to understand what the function is doing since the model built is represented by some learned parameters that mix with the input in some mathematical formula.

This makes it much harder to understand the failure points of the function or model because it is more unclear how a model would behave with unseen inputs. This is particularly difficult with the recent rise in deep learning, as deep learning models are much more of a black-box approach than more simple ML approaches. Since the inner workings of the functions are hard to analyze and understand, it becomes much harder to understand and verify edge cases, as well as understand in what cases the model is likely to fail.

Another consequence of models learning the functions from input and output pairs is that ML models are never 100 percent correct (although they can come pretty close in some types of tasks). This means that organizations need to understand how to manage cases where models predict outputs incorrectly. In some cases, such as recommending new songs, the cost of a bad recommendation is not so high. However, in more serious applications, such as the automatic detection of cancer, a wrong prediction can have drastic consequences, so processes need to be put in place to deal with this.

Deterioration of Models. ML models are called "models" because they are ultimately trying to accurately represent some behavior occurring in the real world. For example, a model that aims to forecast how many ice creams can be sold in a day will be modeling the behavior of ice cream demand across a population.

Say that the temperature on a given day was given as an input to model the impact temperature has on ice cream sales. The model will likely find a positive correlation between temperature and ice cream sales, and sales will, in all likelihood, be predicted relatively accurately.

We all know that the world we live in is incredibly complex and that behaviors change over time. This means that any model trained on historical data will be more and more out of date as the world changes and adapts to new circumstances. In the case of our ice cream model, there could be an increased awareness over time that ice creams are unhealthy because of their sugar content, leading to a slight decrease in ice cream sales over time. Our model would not accurately represent the real world since a day with the same temperature as a day a year ago will lead to fewer sales. This means our model will need to be retrained to capture the change in behavior.

This phenomenon is extremely common across all areas of ML and leads to models needing to be retrained periodically for the accuracy to not deteriorate over time. A more representative example of this in the real world is the example of fraud detection, where criminals are always coming up with new ways to defraud institutions;

hence models need to adapt to be able to detect these new types of fraud. This reality means that a model is never in its "final state," adding another layer of complexity to AI projects.

Hard to Forecast. It may be tempting to think that because one solution to an AI problem worked to solve another problem very similar to your own, this solution will also work on your problem. For example, you may be building an e-commerce store and find an implementation of a recommender system built on another store that has worked well. However, the reality is that the underlying distribution of the data used to train these models is different. Therefore, you will need a different solution for your specific problem.

Consider this example further. On the surface, the data needed to train the recommender system is almost identical. There is a group of products with some product metadata. Next, there are the users, each with their own characteristics. Lastly, there's a set of interactions between users and the products. Even so, the same implementation of a recommender system works for one website but not for another. How can this be?

There could be many explanations for this phenomenon, but ultimately it comes down to the fact that the distributions generating this data are not the same. In layman's terms, people on one website could be completely different from those on the other website, with various purchasing behaviors and motivations. One model might be great at accurately representing the population's behavior on one website but be bad for the other website.

Sometimes you may get lucky, and a slightly different set of the model hyperparameters could be enough to solve your specific problem. Other times, you might need to look for an entirely different algorithm to solve your problem.

Hard to Measure Progress. Even as an experienced data scientist, it can sometimes be very hard to fully understand why a model isn't performing well. Typically a fair amount of manual inspection is required to figure out why some training examples are being predicted inaccurately, which could even mean looking example by example at what features may be confusing the model. This reality means that it is even harder to determine what changes will lead to any significant improvements in performance.

It is possible to struggle for weeks as you run several experiments and tune certain model parameters that result in only a 1 to 2 percent improvement in the model. Until you suddenly discover a new input feature that improves the model by 10 to 20 percent! Progress in an AI project is very chronologically nonlinear, and it can be challenging at the beginning of a project to know when you'll make that breakthrough that will make your model viable to deploy.

I have witnessed many projects where, for weeks, it felt like that breakthrough was coming, to no avail. When is it the time to decide that enough effort has been expended on one solution hypothesis? There are many possible rabbit holes to go down for any solution, making this question very difficult to answer. The "definition of done" is certainly not clear for an ML project, as your team may feel that extra performance can be obtained. But at what cost? It is imperative to come back to business value to determine whether pursuing that extra model performance will deliver any benefit.

Principles for Agile AI Development. While the previous section describes the difficulties of estimating and delivering an AI project relative to a software project, there are some tactics that organizations can implement to give themselves a leg up when it comes to becoming an AI-powered organization (Table 10.2).

Data Science Processes. There are many different ways to implement a data science project. This has led to the creation of some processes that formalize some of the steps required. In this section, we will explore some of these processes.

Table 10.2 Agile AI development

Define your company's mission and near term strategy	This topic was covered extensively in the first section of the chapter, but it is so important that it should be included here again. Not only should you take the time to define this, but once you have it, make sure that the ML applications that you work on directly impact your north star metrics.
Follow the data science hierarchy of needs	The data science hierarchy of needs (Rogati 2017) places AI at the top of the pyramid (think self-actualization if you are familiar with Maslow's hierarchy of needs). Before you can effectively build AI into your organization, crucial aspects need to be developed, such as data collection mechanisms and the ability to run data analytics on your connected data. Figure 10.1 shows the full data science hierarchy of needs that you should follow as a path toward building an AI-driven organization.
Build data labeling into your product	Building labeled data sets for ML applications is expensive, particularly when you must outsource the labeling to external services. If you can build a mechanism in your product that encourages users to label data (e.g., categorizing a transaction in your banking app), you will organically build a large enough dataset to train an ML model.
Make your first AI project a simple one	Andrew Ng, the cofounder of Coursera and Landing.ai, preaches this tactic in his playbook to usher organizations into the world of AI. There are many direct and indirect benefits of working on a simple AI project first, but mainly it (a) delivers immediate value to the organization, (b) secures buy-in from stakeholders that AI is a valuable area to invest in, and (c) delivers a successful project will boost team morale and have knock-on effects for future projects.
Make sure the problem is very well-defined	The more precisely you can describe the problem you're trying to solve, the more you can narrow down approaches that may solve the problem. Consider what edge cases your algorithm might face and how it should approach those. It really helps to try to solve the problem manually first, as a team, so you have a few examples to base your discussion on and start to exclude or include potential solution approaches.
Do the simplest thing that could possibly work	When starting any project (this also applies to non-AI or ML projects), it often helps to refer back to the 80/20 rule and think about the simplest thing. That gets you most of the way there with little development. This tactic has two clear advantages: 1. You may find that the simplest method you can think of already delivers enough value. Otherwise, you have a better idea of how far from the target performance this simple method gets you, which can be useful to understand the complexity of the problem. 2. A simple method will force you to think more about the whole end-to-end solution (data inputs/outputs, pipelines) rather than focus on building a complicated algorithm. This will uncover any unexpected surprises that might arise when deploying this algorithm, and these can be handled in parallel while the algorithm is improved and research is underway.

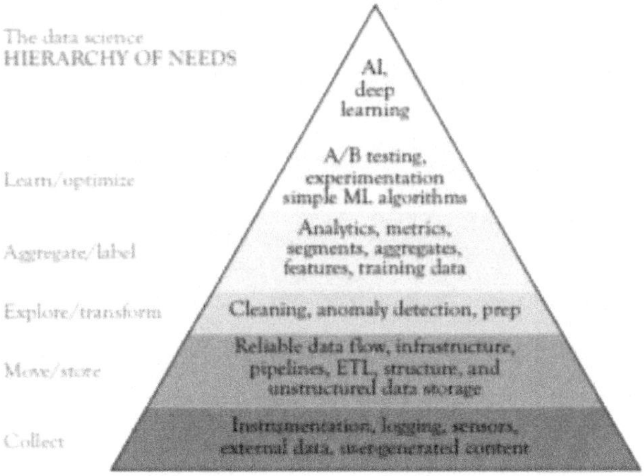

Figure 10.1 Data science Hierarchy of needs

The processes outlined here are all slight variations on each other while following a common set of principles on how to approach data science projects. If you are to take anything from this section, it should be these principles. The final processes should fit your project style and requirements rather than shifting your ways of working to fit these processes. These processes are guidelines and best practices, but real projects are messy so always think about what types of processes will suit your specific set of circumstances.

Process 1: CRISP-DM. CRISP-DM (Cross-Industry Standard Process for Data Mining) is perhaps the most popular process used to plan a typical data science project. The purpose of CRISP-DM is to clearly define the phases that make up a data science project and to understand how those phases interact with each other.

Unlike the Microsoft Team Data Science Process described as follows, CRISP-DM does not concern itself with the lower-level details of how work is managed or the roles and responsibilities in the team. Instead, CRISP-DM is a high-level framework that will help you to understand what kind of work is carried out in each phase of the project and also the deliverables that could be expected. Above all, though, CRISP-DM emphasizes the iterative nature of a data science project and is flexible to move between phases in response to new learnings and findings during the project.

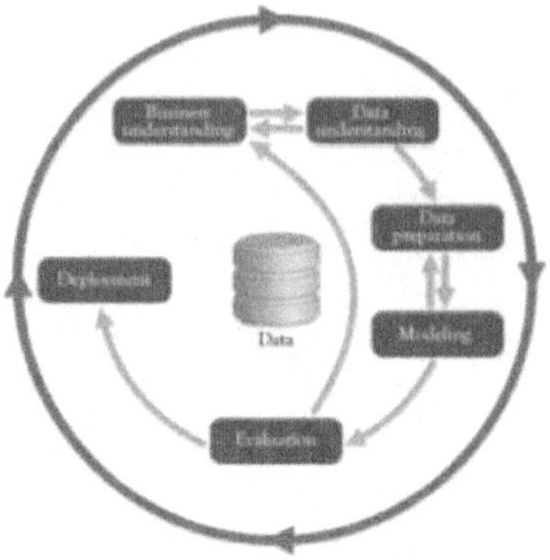

Figure 10.6 Six main phases of the CRISP-DM process

1. Business Understanding
2. Data Understanding
3. Data Preparation
4. Modeling
5. Evaluation
6. Deployment

Business Understanding: The first phase sets out the context for the project by focusing on three main areas: (a) defining the business objectives, (b) identifying the project requirements, and (c) building a project plan. Setting clear business objectives is arguably the most important part of the process because these will be continually referred back to throughout the project to make important decisions. Think about a primary goal that you are seeking to achieve and any related questions that would be useful to address. Once you have these, consider which metrics will most accurately track the progress toward achieving the primary business objective. It is dangerous to define a project outcome that is not measurable as it may lead to a misunderstanding within the team of whether the project is moving in the right direction. Also, it is common for project teams to go down rabbit holes that may not contribute to moving the needle on the business objective, so having metrics to track will be useful to course correct.

What Is A Data Strategy?

Once the business objectives have been agreed upon, consider the key requirements and dependencies for the project. It is best to have a data scientist involved in this process to validate the feasibility of the project with the specified data and resources. The requirements can be split into several categories, such as project resources, data, and computing resources.

While there are many uncertainties at this phase of the project, it can be helpful to draw up a high-level project plan with key milestones you want to hit. As data science projects are quite exploratory and uncertain in nature, make sure to be realistic in your timelines and add a good amount of buffer to avoid unexpected delays.

Data Understanding: This is always the first step of any data scientist when approaching a new problem. The outcome of this phase is to verify that there is enough data and that it is of a high enough quality to build accurate models.
Common pitfalls in the data are variables having lots of missing values, the correct variables not being collected for the project, or there being noise in the data due to some error in the collection process. The data understanding phase should seek to extract these insights and validate any preconceived assumptions about what the data is describing. A typical output of this phase is a report that highlights the findings and any immediate actions that might need to be taken to correct errors in the data.

Data Preparation: The precursor to the modeling phase is the preparation phase. A data scientist will select the appropriate data from the various identified data sources and perform data cleaning and wrangling exercises to transform it into a state that will allow it to be inputted into a data science model.
This phase will be repeated several times throughout the project, as you will undoubtedly learn and experiment with different data points and different processing methods to improve modeling results. You will often hear the phrase "Garbage In, Garbage Out," and this is also true of modeling —often, the best improvements in data science models are generated by carefully selecting the input data and processing it in creative ways rather than fine-tuning the model parameters.

Modeling: The modeling phase involves researching and developing the most appropriate models for the use case. There is a lot of uncertainty in this phase of the project, as models don't always transfer across use cases, even when the use cases are very similar. Owing to this, it is important to start with simple models and then iterate from there as you build up an understanding of the limitations of the simple models. There are many open-source libraries and packages that make it easy to get started with prebuilt models; we have listed a few at the end of the document relating to each use case.

Before beginning any model development, make sure you have a clear understanding of which model evaluation metrics will be used to compare and select the best models, for example do you prioritize precision or recall? This depends vastly on your use case and the cost of different errors. As described previously, the modeling phase and data preparation phase are tightly linked. Each model is based on slightly different assumptions of the data, so the data may need to be processed differently for each model. Furthermore, models can be improved through better feature engineering (which variables you feed into the model from the raw input data).

Evaluation: As opposed to the model evaluation that forms a part of the modeling phase, the evaluation phase here is about determining how well the project is measuring up to the overall business objectives set out at the beginning of the project. At this stage, you will undoubtedly have learned a lot about the data, and the complexities of the project, meaning you may choose to revisit the business objectives slightly based on your learnings.
Perhaps in this stage, it would make sense to test the model in a real, lightweight setting with real users. While the model may be performing well in a development environment, it may not perform as well as you expect in a production environment if the data doesn't quite match real life or if there are any factors that have been overlooked while developing the model.

Deployment: If you get to the stage you are happy with the model results, congratulations! You are almost at the point where you can derive business value from the project. The final stage of the project is the deployment stage, where you must decide how the model will be running in production. Common questions to ask here are:

- How often will the model be run on new data? Batch predictions or real-time?
- How will the model communicate with the input and output systems? Does any API (Application Programming Interface) need to be designed?
- How will you monitor the performance of the model over time? Who will be responsible for this?
- How often does the model need to be retrained? Ideally, this question should be answered during the evaluation phase as you understand how the model performance decays over time.

Process 2: Microsoft Team Data Science Process. Microsoft defines the Team Data Science Process (Microsoft n.d.) as follows:
The Team Data Science Process (TDSP) is an agile, iterative data science methodology to deliver predictive analytics solutions and intelligent applications efficiently. TDSP helps improve team collaboration and learning by suggesting how team roles work best together. TDSP includes best practices and structures from Microsoft and other industry leaders to help toward the successful implementation of data science initiatives. The goal is to help companies fully realize the benefits of their analytics program.

The process is defined by the following key components:
1. A data science life cycle definition.
2. A standardized project structure.
3. Infrastructure and resources for data science projects.
4. Tools and utilities for project execution.

For the context of what we've been discussing in this chapter, the data science life cycle definition is the most relevant. Components 2 to 4 are incredibly useful when getting to the implementation, and I encourage you to check it out on Microsoft's website. For the rest of this section, we'll only focus on the life cycle.
The life cycle defined in this project borrows a lot from the CRISP-DM methodology described in the last section but reinforces the importance of making the process iterative and, above all, iterating between each main phase of the project rather than only iterating through the full cycle. The life cycle can be summarized by the following diagram (Figure 10.3).
As you can see from the diagram, the four main phases of the life cycle are:

- Business Understanding
- Data Acquisition and Understanding
- Modeling
- Deployment

This can be mapped almost like-for-like to CRISP-DM, with the only exceptions being that Data Understanding and Data Preparation have been collapsed into Data Acquisition and Understanding, and Modeling and Evaluation have been collapsed into Modeling. Given this similarity, please refer to the previous section for detailed explanations on the kind of activities carried out in each phase.

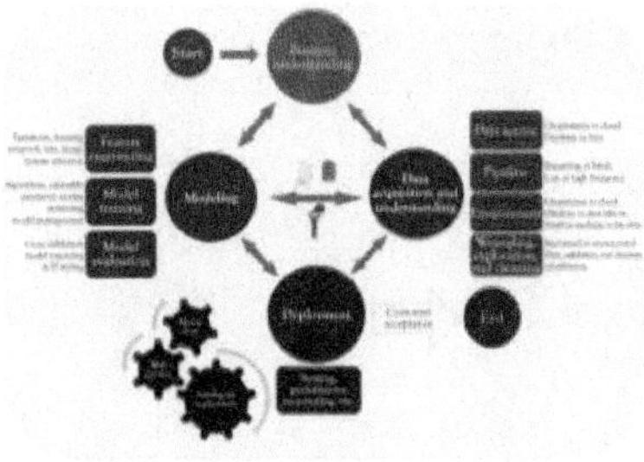

Figure 3.3 Data science life cycle

The important area to emphasize in this section is the iterative nature of the process. Being agile in the way you approach data science development will undoubtedly give you an advantage in delivering quality projects on time. It is very rare to go through the process once. It would mean having the perfect problem definition, knowing exactly what data you need to solve the problem, and then developing and deploying the perfect model. That doesn't happen. There will be surprises and lessons along the way that will change previously held assumptions in the process.

In the Business Understanding phase, you will come up with an initial plan for how you're going to solve the problem that you've set out and what data you will need to train a model. Once the plan is created, the first step is to explore the data you have identified to see if the quality and quantity are sufficient. The findings from this phase will provide some new information, such as whether there is any missing data for the data points you wish to extract or whether there is an imbalance of training examples (e.g., the majority of your users are male; therefore, your algorithm might suffer in accuracy for female users). It is vital to revisit the documents prepared in the Business Understanding phase to update the assumptions and the proposed approaches.

Likewise, the modeling phase might prove that some method of approaching the problem is infeasible, which would need updating in the Business Understanding documents.
However, the most common feedback loop from the diagram is the interaction between the Data Acquisition and Understanding phase and the Modeling phase. As explained in the AI Principles section, starting with the simplest model you can think of on a small subset of your entire data is beneficial. The model will likely not be very accurate. However, exploring the model's errors may give you a clue as to what other data points will help it improve.

For example, I worked on a project where we were building recommender systems to recommend books to children. We found, from initial models, that the recommendations were irrelevant for children since their preferences change so quickly as they grow up. From this, we were able to identify that knowing the child's age would improve the model considerably by making more age-specific recommendations.

Over the lifetime of a project, there will be many iterations across this loop, and you want to make sure that you record the findings along the way so that you have some traceability of the data points that have been tested and what approaches have worked or not worked.

Lastly, once you have a satisfactory model and are ready to deploy, there will be some back and forth between the Deployment phase and the Modeling and Data Acquisition and Understanding phases as you try to discover the optimal approach to deploying a model. The model will need to access new data from your production databases, so you need to consider how and where the data is stored and where the predictions of the model will be stored. Similarly, will the model be deployed through an API or run as a scheduled job to train and output new predictions? The response to this may require some changes in the Modeling phase to ensure the model is suitable for your requirements.

Microsoft has released a Github repository that anyone can use to get started with the process:

https://github.com/Azure/Azure-TDSPProjectTemplate.
Process 3: Tesseract Academy's 2-Actor Process. Tesseract Academy's 2-actor process focuses not so much on how the data strategy interacts with the business but more on the interpersonal dynamics between the data scientist and the business leader.
The previous processes do a good job of breaking down the steps required to complete a data science project. Tesseract Academy's process takes a more person-centric view, focusing a lot on the challenges and misinterpretations that can take place between the two main actors of any data science project: the key business stakeholder and the data science lead. This process is an excellent complement to the other processes outlined here and can help you uncover any challenges that might arise.

The process assumes that a company does not have a data science function and can be very useful for organizations embarking on that journey. Companies that have been working with data for a long time will find that many of the challenges outlined in this process might not exist for them.
In this process, there are two main actors and four steps. The main actors are the domain expert (or key business stakeholder) and the data scientist (or, in the case of a data science team, the team leader).

The four steps are outlined as follows.
Under each step, you will find the person who is responsible for completing it.

1. Problem definition
a. Domain expert

2. Choosing the right data (data management)
a. Domain expert
b. Data scientist

3. Solution of the problem
a. Data scientist

4. Creating value through actionable insights
a. Data scientist AND domain expert

Problem definition: This is where the key problem is defined. This is done by the domain expert (and key business stakeholder). Why is it the domain expert instead of the data scientist? Because no one can speak better about the problems of the business than someone who is actually part of the business. While a data scientist might bring some external knowledge, the domain expert is the one who should really understand all the intricacies of their organization.

This means that they should be able to pose a list of relevant problems/challenges.
The data scientist may have worked in this field before and might have some great ideas, which can be used straight out of the box. However, even if that's the case, the domain expert needs to have at least a clear idea of the business problems to really own the proposed solution and prioritize any suggestions accordingly.

There is no requirement here to be 100 percent specific. For example, a domain expert who lacks an understanding of data science might find it challenging to provide an unambiguous description of the business's problems. That's fine, as long as they can give an accurate picture of the overall business and some key performance indicators.
The danger here is being vague and unable to explain what the expected key metrics or results are to the data scientist. Solving the challenge requires the data scientist to make sure they are optimizing for the right target and then communicating these results to the domain expert so that the benefit becomes clear. This first step is crucial in achieving this goal.

Choosing the right data (data management): This is tricky because it requires the synergy of both the data scientist and the domain expert. In an ideal world, the business has followed a data strategy from day zero. The data is clean and of good quality. The domain is relatively simple, and there is no noise in the data. Unfortunately, this is the exception rather than the rule.

In most cases, a business will not have followed a data strategy. This means that the data scientist might encounter many issues, such as:

1. Missing values;
2. Important and useful variables not being collected;
3. Data being collected at the wrong level of granularity (e.g., month instead of day).

Similarly, there is a significant danger here coming from the domain. One of the authors worked with a company producing a radar device. He developed an algorithm for them, but when the company changed the chipset, the algorithm stopped working. The problem was due to the noise inherent in the two chipsets and some other version differences in the hardware. Both the author and the company were unaware that upgrading the chipset wouldn't improve the algorithm, but rather it would require complete retraining. So, the best way to walk through this step is through a back-and-forth between the data scientist and the domain expert. Make no assumptions! Do not assume that the data is correct, accurate, or lacks noise. Be very skeptical of any early, very successful results. It is more likely that you have data leakage rather than amazing data.
An example of data leakage is when an input variable correlates very highly with the outcome variable but wouldn't usually be available at the test time. For example, if you are forecasting quarterly sales and someone is adding a binary variable indicating whether sales were high or low, this would cause performance to spike. But this variable was created after looking into the past.
Solution of the problem: This step comes down to the data scientist. If the previous steps have been done correctly, the following things will be in place:
1. A clear definition of the problem and the business.
2. A good, clean set of data.

The data scientist now needs to do the following:
1. Identify the key metrics of success.
2. Solve the problem using a variety of data science methods.

This takes us to step 4.
Creating value through actionable insights: So far, the domain expert–data scientist duo have achieved the following:
1. Built a common understanding of the problem.
2. Checked the quality of the data.
3. Created a solution.

Now it's time for the two actors to work in complete synergy. The data scientist has to explain to the domain expert how the solution really addresses the problem outlined in step 1. The decision maker has to understand and approve this solution. The solution needs to be translated in measurable results. This way, the domain expert can integrate it into the overall company strategy, and the data scientist can have a measure of performance to use as a benchmark when further improving the solution.

Case Studies

Let's take a look at a few case studies to make all the above easier to understand.

Case Study 1: The Recommender System

A recommender system is an invaluable tool for any e-commerce business and beyond. Spotify uses a recommender system to best identify the songs you are going to like. Amazon is using a recommender system to recommend products to you. And Netflix uses a recommender system to try and predict what movies or shows you will watch for hours.
So, in this case study, we will deal with a fictional company called Zookla. Zookla is an online retailer of sports clothes and equipment. The company consists of 10 people and includes software developers, business development, and the CEO, who is still very much involved in day-to-day operations. The company recently raised $5 million and wants to establish a data science function. The first thing they care most about is creating a recommender system.
Zookla hires a data scientist to deal with this on a six-month contract.
Analysis: Tesseract Academy's 2-Actor Model We will analyze the project from the perspective of Tesseract Academy's 2-actor model. Here is a reminder of the process:

1. Problem definition
a. Domain expert

2. Choosing the right data (data management)
a. Domain expert
b. Data scientist

3. Solution of the problem
a. Data scientist

4. Creating value through actionable insights
a. Data scientist AND domain expert
So, let's see the good and the bad scenario for each step.

Problem Definition: Good Scenario
In a good scenario, the CEO has a good idea of what a recommender system is and how it could improve profits. The CEO also has a good idea of what this would look like on the screen. There are many ways to present a recommender system. For example, Amazon uses the following two ways: "frequently bought together" and "customers who bought this also bought," As depicted in Figure 10.4.

Figure 10.4 Example of the Amazon recommender system in action.

Figure 10.5 Examples of the Spotify recommender system in action.

Spotify, on the other hand, creates custom playlists based on the songs you like, as shown in Figure 10.5.. And obviously, there are many other ways to present recommendations, such as a list or tiles (e.g., Netflix).

The way recommendations are presented interacts with the UI/UX (User Interface/User Experience). And the way the UX/UI is designed affects how the data is collected. It's essential to be aware of these interplays. Also, finally, it helps if the CEO has good intuition or the company has done some preliminary research on useful patterns (e.g., customer segmentation). These can not only help inform the design of a recommender system but they can also be used to create a simple rule-based recommender that could be used as a benchmark for a more advanced version.

Problem Definition: Bad Scenario

In the bad scenario, the CEO falls into one of these two groups:

1. They say they "want to do something useful with data," but they are not sure what that is.

2. They say they want a recommender system, but they are oblivious to all the details and issues that this entails.

The first scenario is pretty common and most data scientists would be prepared for it. In this case, the data scientist will take some time to explain data science to the CEO, learn more about the business, and discover the best way forward. The CEO would have been better off if they had done this preparatory work before hiring a data scientist because the result is one to two months of work.

The second case is much trickier. The CEO might be confident in what they want, but they might be ignoring a lot of critical topics:

1. They might be ignoring the interaction between the recommender system and UX/UI in how results are displayed and how data are collected.

2. They have no real understanding of their customers.

3. They are not sure what metrics they are after. What would success look like for this project?

So, the first point can be a huge problem if, for example, the website requires an extensive redesign to display recommendations and collect relevant data. Points 2 and 3 often come together. Sometimes, there is lots of enthusiasm about a project, but the client does not really know what they're looking for. Is it simply more sales? More engagement? How much more?
It is not possible to forecast the level of success. However, it is not uncommon for a project to finish and for the client to realize they are not happy with the results because they couldn't verbalize their expectations from the onset. For example, if a client believes that a recommender system would double sales, this is likely unrealistic. The data scientist could explain what might be more feasible or how they could create a constantly improving system.
There are cases where clients hold latent beliefs about the expectations surrounding new AI systems, but even they are not aware of them until the last minute when things don't seem to be going the way they wanted them to go.

Case Study 2: Forecasting Demand

Forecasting demand is a common problem in industries like retail. If a business can successfully do it, it can optimize its supply chains and orders to maximize margins. Let's take the example of Leotard Clothes. This is a retailer that sells cat-inspired clothes.
They have limited space in their warehouses, and producing clothes takes a significant amount of time and resources due to the special fabrics used. Also, they use many outside contractors, which means that costs will vary according to manufacturing volume. Manufacturing more clothes than the demand will significantly increase monthly costs, but if they manufacture fewer clothes, the company can still make a profit. Another issue with contractors is that there were shortages of material in some cases. Leotard Clothes would ideally like to preorder fabric a few months in advance.

Hence for them, predicting demand is vital so that they know how many clothes to manufacture each month.
Let's see how Leotard Clothes can use the CRISP-DM approach to forecast demand.

Analysis: CRISP-DM

Let's revisit the CRISP-DM process. Six main phases are described as part of the CRISP-DM process (Figure 10.6):
1. Business Understanding
2. Data Understanding

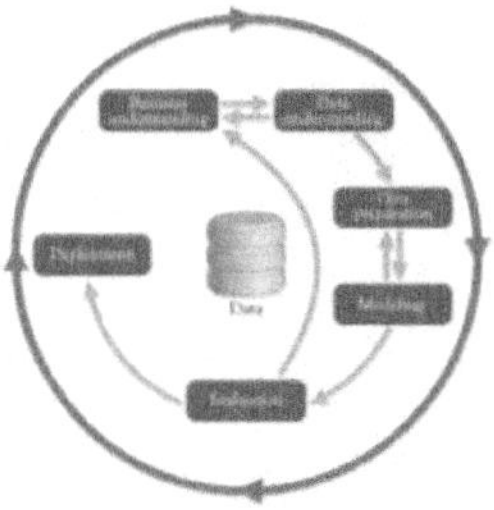

Figure 10.7 Example of the Teams Data Science Process=

3. Data Preparation
4. Modeling
5. Evaluation
6. Deployment

The first step (business understanding) is key. While forecasting is what the company wants to do, it wants to do this within the context of its operations. This means that forecasting demand is being used to optimize the allocation of resources. This step is directly connected to the fifth step (evaluation). Why is that? Because when evaluating a ML pipeline, we need to identify how results are translated into business actions. Since forecasting is a regression problem, the reported metrics will be something like the Mean Absolute Error or the Root Mean Squared Error. But what is a good score? This is very much business related. There are domains where a difference of 1 percent in performance can translate into millions of dollars. In other fields, a difference of 5 percent might not mean much. In this particular example, the interest is in ensuring the following:

1. There is enough space in the warehouse.
2. Point 1 requires that the clothes are sold, and there is enough demand.
3. Point 1 also requires that the materials ordered align with the demand.

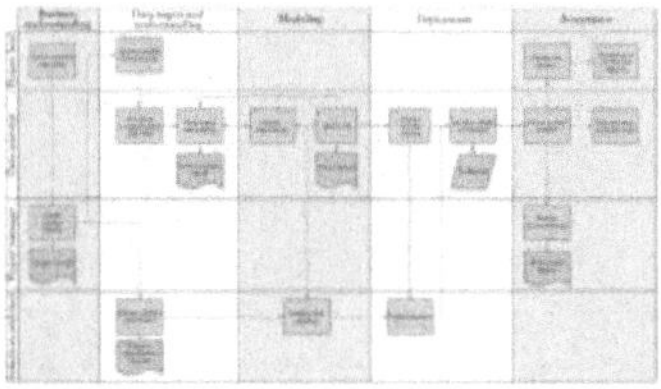

Figure 10.6 Six main phases of the CRISP-DM process

Hence, while we are predicting demand, the key challenge is how to make sure that the warehouse has enough space.

So, this should be our main focus. The rest of the steps in CRISP-DM are pretty standard in any data science project. Most data scientists will follow a similar process, even if they do not explicitly phrase it. We leave the analysis here because the Teams Data Science Process (discussed in Figure 10.7) covers some of these steps in greater depth.

Case Study 3: Natural Language Processing

Let's see how we could use the Teams Data Science Process to break down a given problem. Suppose we are dealing with an online clothes retailer called Zappo. The company is interested in running natural language processing on its social media accounts to better understand how they could be improved.

The first thing we notice is that there are four actors:

1. Project lead
2. Data scientist
3. Project manager
4. Solution architect

According to the process, the solution architect is responsible for ensuring a proper business understanding within the company. The process also defines some technical tasks that need to be achieved. For example, in the first step, the repository is created by the project lead instead of the data scientist, hence clearly separating responsibilities between the different roles.

In our case, the project lead needs to define what would be measured. For example, the company could choose to measure:

1. Sentiment analysis on user comments about its products.
2. Prediction of post engagement.
3. Time series analysis of engagement metrics.

So, we can immediately see that a general task of "using NLP to study social media" immediately breaks down into multiple different tasks. Each task should be treated separately. So, we can assume that the company in this use case decided to focus on the first task and go with sentiment analysis.

The second stage of the process involves the data scientist, who is responsible for producing a report. You can see that the first output of the data scientist is something that can be easily communicated to the management. The process clearly places significant emphasis on business understanding. At the same time, the solution architect will start working on the deployment specifics. In our case, this would be about the choice of database, setting up APIs to extract data from social media, and so on.

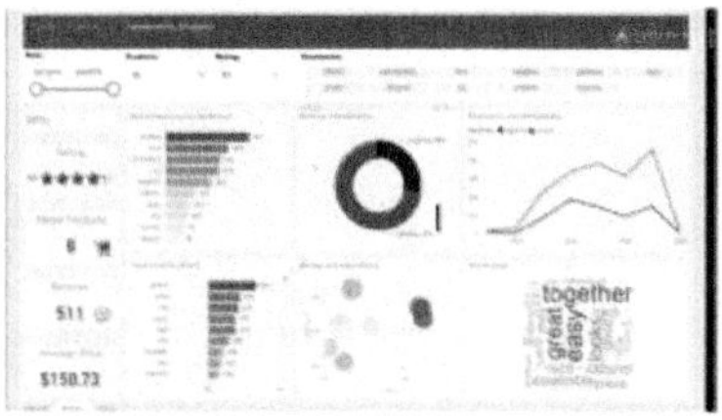

Figure 10.8 A sentiment analysis dashboard
Source: Faction A 2018

The third step, modeling, consists of the data scientist running various sentiment analyses algorithms and comparing them. The output of this stage is a model report. Again, this helps keep track of how the project is progressing and communicating value to the business stakeholders.

The fourth step is deployment. In the third and the fourth steps, the main actors are the data scientist and the solution architect. The results, in this case, are communicated through a dashboard. The dashboard in our example could contain things such as classifications of reviews and a word cloud (Figure 10.8).

In the final stage, acceptance, the project lead and the project manager come back into play and bring everything together. A final report, written by the project manager, ensures that everything has been documented and the project can be finalized.

Case Study 4: Computer Vision and Algorithmic Bias
This case study will investigate three interesting challenges: computer vision, algorithmic bias, and data privacy.
Let's say that you are developing a piece of software that can extract information about the people in a retail store by using cameras installed in the store. This application can be used to calculate not only footfall but also the characteristics of the different people in the store, such as gender, age, race, and so on.

You have decided that you will use a commoditized solution for computer vision such as Google Vision or IBM Watson.

Something important to note here is that this is a special case. The reason is that this use case also touches upon issues of compliance, regulation, and ethics. Let's see why:
First, the company will have to make sure that the individuals' private data is not stored. This refers to the actual images or inferences made about an individual, such as age. It is likely that,

depending on the geographical region, the exact legal requirements will be different, but there will undoubtedly be various legal complications.

Secondly, the application should make sure that it is not biased against certain types of people. It is well known that computer vision algorithms can be biased against minorities. A famous article by Time demonstrated how a computer vision API might mistake Oprah Winfrey for a man, for example ("Artificial Intelligence Has a Problem With Gender and Racial Bias" n.d.).

Given that the main challenges here touch upon different parts of the business, Tesseract Academy's 2-actor model could be very useful. The benefit of this model is that it is very flexible, so it can also be applied in circumstances where the challenge is not only of a technical nature. The key point behind this process is that it lays out all the challenges that the project might face. Therefore, the decision maker and the data scientist can make sure they are on the same page when tackling a particular challenge.

Analysis: Tesseract Academy's 2-Actor Model
So, let's revisit the process.
1. Problem definition
a. Domain expert

2. Choosing the right data
a. Domain expert
b. Data scientist

3. Solution of the problem
a. Data scientist

Problem Definition.
In this particular case, the core problem definition is clear. The business owner wants to know specific statistics about the people in a store, such as gender, age, and race.

However, the core problem definition needs to be extended. We also need to add:
1. Data privacy
2. Elimination of bias

These points are going to inform the solution to the problem. The decision maker has also defined that the business should go for a commoditized solution, instead of developing their own solution internally.

Choosing the Right Data. In this case, the data is a direct feed coming from cameras located inside the store. Therefore, the cameras must be of high quality, and the network must have enough bandwidth to feed the data to the API.

Data privacy falls under this step. Remember that data management involves both the decision-maker and the data scientist. While the data scientist is responsible for the technical aspects, the decision maker needs to ensure that the business is compliant.

What they both need to decide upon is how the data can be fed to the API and what are the implications of the different choices. Is the data going to be stored somewhere and then sent? Or is it going to be sent in real time? How does this affect costs for data storage and network usage?

Solution to the Problem. Given the extended problem definition and the constraints imposed by the decision maker, the data scientist has to define the right solution and come up with an attack plan. In this case, the attack plan does not involve data analysis but rather the comparison of different solutions in the market.

More specifically, the data scientist will have to run A/B tests between all major computer vision service providers and identify which ones seem to work best. The data scientist might have to go to the store and test these systems in real time in realistic conditions.

Creating Value Through Actionable Insights. Typically, actionable insights are derived after data has been analyzed. In this case, the data scientist and the decision maker will have to constantly monitor the system or the first few months of operation to ensure it works as expected. All sorts of problems could arise that could affect the result, but that might not be related to the API, such as issues with the cameras. The following Table 10.3 summarizes all of the above insights.

Problem definition	1. Get statistics 2. Data privacy 3. No bias
Choosing the right data (data management)	1. Data feed from cameras 2. Data privacy
Solution of the problem	1. Discover the best API 2. Test APIs in realistic conditions
Creating value through actionable insights	1. Ensure that the API works as expected 2. Revisit the model if required

Table 10.3 Summary of Tesseract Academy's 2-actor model

Key Takeaways

· Data strategy is defined as "a living document that defines how the business is setting itself up, both from a technical and organizational perspective, to proactively manage and leverage data towards the long-term business strategy."

· Data science development is different to software development. Managing a data science project requires following a data science process.

· There are different processes for data science, some popular ones being CRISP-DM and the Tesseract Academy's 2-actor process.

A Short Introduction To Statistics

CHAPTER 11

Statistics has two branches, namely, descriptive statistics and inferential statistics.

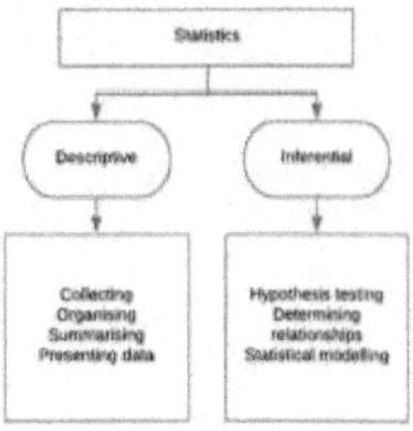

Figure 11-1. **The two branches of the science of statistics**

Descriptive statistics is what most people associate with the word statistics. These are things that you've probably done in high school. They include things like collecting data, using summary metrics such as the mean, and visualizing data.
Inferential statistics is what most statisticians think of when they think of the word statistics. It involves more advanced concepts such as sampling and inferring the values of the parameters of the population.

Descriptive Statistics

Descriptive statistics deals with organizing, summarizing, and presenting data in a convenient and informative way. Two sets of methods are used in this type of statistics.

First, there are numerical methods for describing the data. These include measures for the location of the data, like mean, median, and mode. They also include measures of the variability of the data, such as the range, variance, and standard deviation.

The second set of methods cover graphical means of presenting data, which you probably know quite well, such as bar charts, pie charts, histograms, and so on.
I like to refer to descriptive statistics as "high school statistics." The reason is that most people are taught descriptive statistics in high school and they think that descriptive statistics are representative of the overall field of statistical science. However, the truth is much different.

Inferential Statistics

When a statistician is talking about statistics, this is usually what they refer to. Inferential statistics is much more interesting and useful than descriptive statistics. It basically represents 90% of statistics, with descriptive statistics representing merely the tip of the iceberg.
Thus, inferential statistics is a body of methods used to draw conclusions or inferences about the characteristics of a population based on sample data.

A Short Introduction To Statistics

Some of the fundamental terminology used in inferential statistics includes

- Data, elements, variables, and observations
- Population—The group of all the items a statistician is interested in
- Sample—A set of data drawn from the population
- Parameter—A descriptive measure of a population
- Statistic—A descriptive measure of a sample
- Inference—A set of methods, such as estimation, testing, and prediction, used to draw conclusions or inferences about the traits of a population based on data from a sample

So, what does this all mean? What does inferential statistics actually do?
Inferential statistics allows us to quantify uncertainty. In other words, let's say you want to find out something about a population. Let's go with something simple, like the average height of the people in a country.

Now, to determine this figure, the first thought would be that you have to take every person in that country to determine their height. Or, measure every person. When a country has a population of 50 million, that isn't going to be an easy undertaking. Even for something so simple, you are going to be spending a lot of time and money trying to talk to every person. Studying every individual is, at the very least, impractical, but in most cases impossible.

With inferential statistics, you can take a sample of the population and express uncertainty through a probability distribution. It helps us turn the uncertainty into a quantifiable metric, which then allows us to run calculations. This is what allows us to do statistical modeling and hypothesis testing.

So, essentially, what happens is that you can take a sample of 1000 people, for example, and extrapolate their average height to the entire population of 50 million. And working with a thousand people is much, much easier than trying to work with 50 million.

This idea of expressing uncertainty using a probability distribution is a simple, but extremely powerful idea. Humanity owes a lot to the founding fathers of statistics, people such as Ronald Fischer, Jerzy Neyman, and Karl Pearson who came up with methods such as ANOVA and multiple linear regression and built up the mathematical foundations of much of modern statistics.

Without inferential statistics, most sciences would lack the tools to make informed decisions. Every time you hear about a study in medicine, psychology, economics, or otherwise, you should know this is possible due to inferential statistics.

A Short Introduction To Statistics

How to Use Statistics

Okay, so now it's time to look at how you can use statistics. Once again, we'll be taking a high-level view and won't be looking at it from a statistician's or data scientist's perspective, but from a non-technical decision maker's perspective. First of all, it's likely that you're already using descriptive statistics in some shape or form.

Metrics like the mean and the median or plots and graphs like bar charts and histograms are something that most people can relate to. However, it's important to be aware of some of the pitfalls that could pop up, which we will discuss in greater detail a little later.

Then you have inferential statistics, which is useful in two situations. It can be used to answer particular questions about variable importance, but also to answer questions about differences in population. By the end of the section, you should understand that statistics is always used to make a case supporting a hypothesis or story, and this involves the extensive use of descriptive statistics. While inferential statistics will often be employed in the analysis, it tends to be with descriptive statistics.

Thus, you as an executive, manager, founder, or decision maker need to be able to understand whether you can use statistics to answer a question and whether the story makes sense and to avoid all the pitfalls and fallacies that can be involved in statistical inference and the presentation of results.

Examples of Inferential Statistics
Let's start with a few examples of inferential statistics to give you a better idea of the concept itself but also to see how you can apply them to your business.

Hypothesis testing and statistical modeling are the two main things you will be using inferential statistics for. Forecasting is another area and represents a set of tools and methods that allow for the prediction of future values. However, we won't be going into forecasting because it is a little more technical and advanced, and it can often be accomplished using machine learning.

Hypothesis Testing
Hypothesis testing is generally used for two things, namely, finding out the value of a population parameter or making comparisons. Determining the value of a population essentially means finding out something like the average height of a population or what their average income is.

Comparisons, on the other hand, involve exploring differences and/or similarities among similar parameters. For example, you could explore differences based on gender, comparing whether men earn more money than women in the same job.

Hypothesis testing is an extremely important tool for science. Every time, for example, you hear about clinical trials for new drugs, a hypothesis test is being employed to detect whether any significant effect is observed. When conducting hypothesis testing, we are essentially comparing two hypotheses: the null hypothesis and the alternative hypothesis. So, in the context of a clinical trial, the null hypothesis would be that a new drug has no effect on a disease.

The hypothesis test produces something called a p-value. This is the probability of the null hypothesis being true, given the data. If the p-value is low (usually we use a 5% threshold), then we reject the null hypothesis and accept the alternative hypothesis.

In business you mainly encounter hypothesis testing in the context of A/B testing. So, when someone is testing two headlines against each other to see which generates the highest click-through rate, for example, they are conducting a comparison-based hypothesis test.

See Table 11-1 for examples of statistical tests.

Table 11-1. Some examples of statistical tests.

Name	Use
T-test	Used to test the equality of the means between two groups
ANOVA	Used to test the equality of the means of multiple groups
Test of proportions	Used to test the equality of proportions in two groups
Wilcoxon signed rank test	Non-parametric alternative to the t-test
Smirnov-Kolmogorov test	Used to test whether a variable is normally distributed
Friedman test	Non-parametric alternative to ANOVA

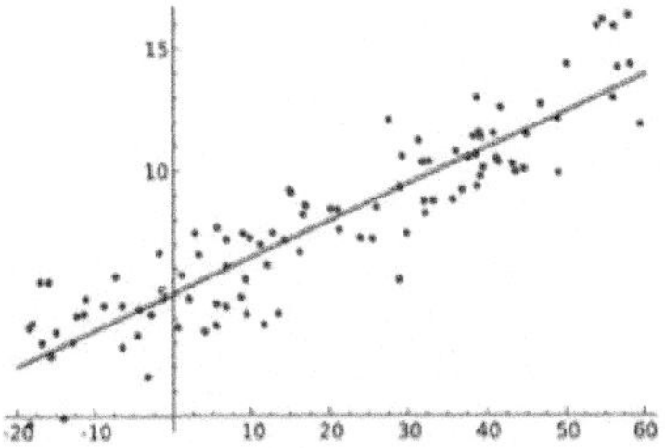

Figure 11-2. Example of simple linear regression

Statistical Modeling

Statistical modeling is used mainly when you are interested to determine whether one variable influences another.

For example, let's say that you've conducted the hypothesis test regarding men earning more money than women in the same position and have come to the conclusion that the statement is accurate. However, you want to discover what other variables might affect income. To achieve this, you turn to statistical modeling.

Figure **11-2** shows an example of linear regression, the most famous statistical model.

So, you enter these variables into the model and discover that income is also affected by age, experience, previous employment, and more. You can also find out to what degree these variables affect the response variable—or the variable of interest—which is income level in our case.
Have you ever heard of linear regression, logistic regression, or the generalized linear model? All these are examples of statistical models. These models form the basis of models used in other more specialized fields such as econometrics and psychometrics. See Table **11-2.**

Table 11-2. Examples of statistical models

Name	Use
Multiple linear regression	Most common statistical model, used when the response variable is numerical
Poisson regression	Used when the target variable consists of positive integers
Logistic regression	Used for binary outcome variables, e.g., understanding the differences between two types of customers
Survival modeling	Used when we care about the time something will take until it fails, e.g., a mechanical part
Log-linear model	Model used to examine the relationship between more than two categorical variables

Misleading with Statistics

People tend to trust statistics blindly and this can be a problem. It's natural to be accepting of what seems like complete facts, especially when they are supported with lots of figures and charts and so on. However, the fact is that statistics can be used to deceive people. They can also lead to skewed results because of mistakes.

This section is essential because statistics is used in the wrong way quite often. We'll look at cases where statistics are being abused, and it's important for you to become aware of the many ways things can go wrong and also of the cases when people are trying to deceive you. This way, you'll be in a position to make better informed decisions.

Lying with Charts

So, let's start with one my favorite ways to mislead with statistics which is to blatantly lie using charts that contain spurious correlations and seem to make sense on the surface, but in reality, they don't make any sense at all.

Take a look at Figures 11-3 and 11-4. Figure 6-3 shows a correlation between the number of people who drowned by falling into a pool and the number of films Nicolas Cage appeared in. Figure 6-4 correlates US spending on science, space, and technology with suicides by hanging, strangulation, and suffocation.

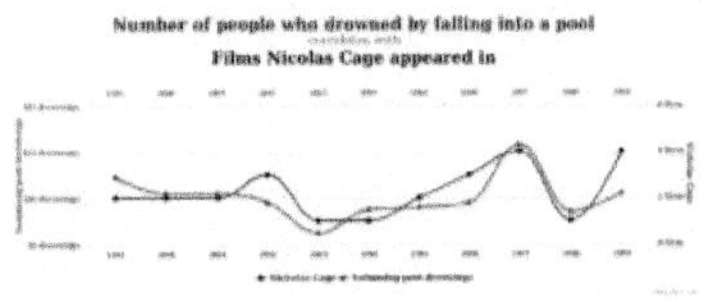

Figure 11-3. Nicolas Cage seems to be driving swimming pool drownings worldwide

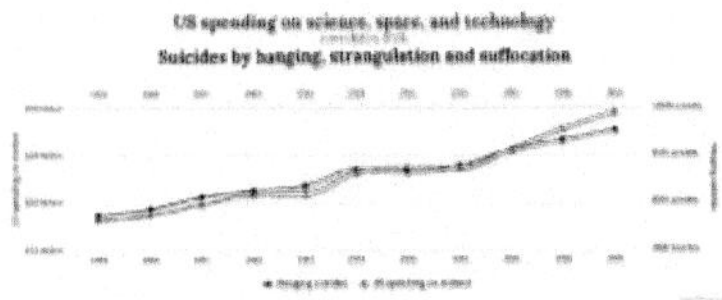

Figure 11-4. US spending on science, space, and technology correlates with suicides by hanging, strangulation, and suffocation.

Now, at first glance, these might look like interesting statistics. The first chart seems to imply that more people drowned when Nicolas Cage starred in more films. Based on this chart alone and without the understanding that statistics can be misleading, you might conclude that people may have actually killed themselves to get away from Nicolas Cage movies. The second chart implies that US spending on science, space, and technology has increased as the number of suicides by hanging, strangulation, and suffocation increased. So, you could draw the conclusion that investing in R&D is a sure way to increase deaths in the overall population!

When you write out the conclusions, it's easier to realize that they really don't make a lot of sense. And yes, these are extreme examples to show how statistics can be used to mislead, but many similar examples exist where the correlations are spurious, even if it's not that obvious, which is why you need to be careful. So, what does it mean that the correlations are spurious? It means that two variables are correlated but the underlying theory as to what's happening doesn't exist. They are simply two variables with no real connection that have been correlated. And let's not forget that correlation does not imply
causation.

In other words, the number of Nicolas Cage movies has absolutely no connection with pool drownings in the real world, making it a spurious correlation. Conversely, if we were to compare Nicolas Cage's earnings with the number of movies he starred in, then the correlation would make sense because there is a connection between the two.

The second chart goes even further in its attempt to trick people because the X-axis has been reversed. In other words, the numbers decrease along the axis instead of increasing, despite the fact that the Y-axis has values that increase as you go higher. This is an attempt to further force a correlation. So, statistics is a great tool, but it isn't a magic wand that can provide answers no matter what. Using statistics also doesn't mean that you can get away with not having the right research design. You also need to have the right framework when looking into problems.

If you want to see more examples of spurious correlations, visit: http:// tylervigen.com/.

It's actually quite funny because in all these correlations, the mistake is always the same, namely, that the theory behind the two variables being studied is not there.

Remember, just because there seems to be a high correlation between the two variables, it doesn't actually mean that the two are related. The problem is that while all these examples have spurious correlations, there are many situations where it isn't quite as obvious.

For example, let's say that there's a high correlation between the amount of time someone has lived with diabetes and the number of people who die before they turn 60. On the surface, without digging deep, you might conclude that the longer someone has had diabetes, the more likely they are to die before they turn 60. It makes for a pretty chart and everything.

However, if you start digging deeper, you discover that the deaths include a wide range of causes, including car crashes, murders, suicides, and so on. In other words, part of the second variable is completely unrelated, even if part is. The
result is the same though, namely, that the decision maker studying a chart like that will come to the wrong conclusion.

Another way to lie with charts is to use different kinds of scales. In the example in Figure 6-5, we have two charts with two bars each, representing type A and type B. Both charts use log scales without explicitly stating they are doing so. Now, by using different scales, you can make two items appear closer to each other than they actually are.

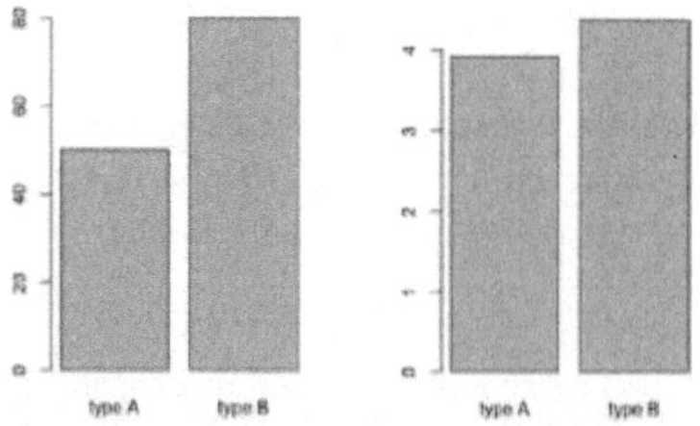

Figure 11-5. Example of how a logarithmic scale can skew perception of the differences between groups

Another easy way to lie with charts is to play around with the scale. For example, in **Figure 11-6** you can see how the image on the left shows a rising trend and the image on the right shows a more or less stable trend. The data is the same in both cases. The only difference is the degree of zoom.

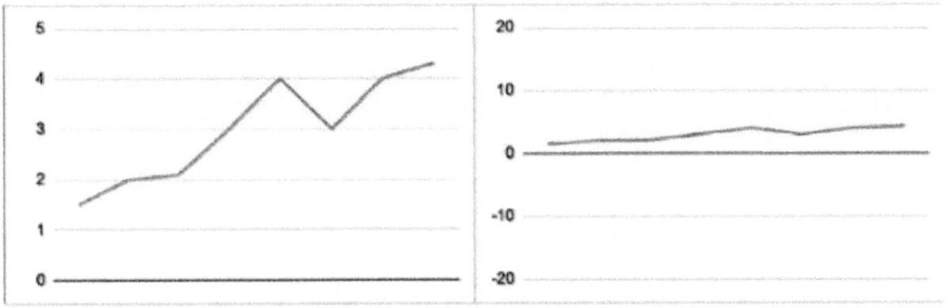

Figure 11-6. Same data, different view

Misleading Using Descriptive Statistics

Now, let's take a look at how you can mislead someone using descriptive statistics. One way to easily lie is by using measures of centrality and summary metrics. There are, in essence, three main measures of centrality, namely, the mean, the median, and the mode.

The mean is the average of a set of numbers, namely, where you add all the numbers together and divide by how many numbers there are. The median s the middle value in a list of numbers, while the mode is the value that occurs most frequently in a list.

Now, in a symmetrical distribution, the mean, median, and mode fall on the same point. However, when we have a positive skew, the mean is lighter than the median, and the median is lighter than the mode, and the opposite happens in a negatively skewed distributions. See Figure 11-7.

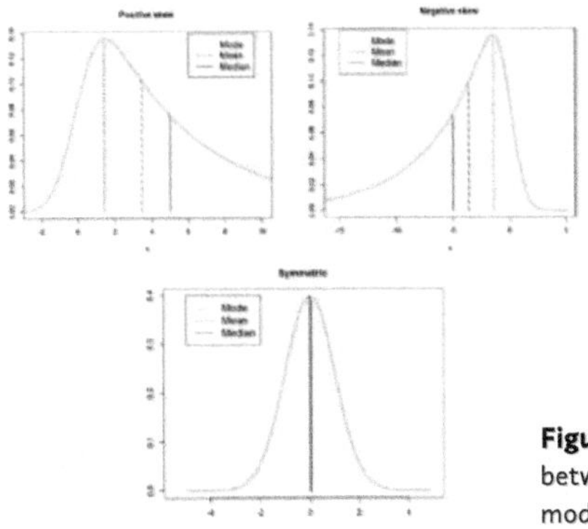

Figure 11-7. Skewness and the relationship between the mean, the median, and the mode

This is important because many distributions in real life are not symmetrical. For example, let's say there is a company where the CEO earns $300K per year, while the rest of the employees—a total of ten—earn $50K per year.
Depending on the image you want to project, you can present different figures. For example, in our situation, the median is $50K per year, but the mean is $72K per year.
A malicious company might advertise the mean salary as being $72K per year when looking to hire someone, but in reality, they aren't willing to pay employees other than the CEO anything over $50K. But this way, they could trick somebody into thinking they could eventually make $72K per year, and they wouldn't even have to come out and say it like that as the figures imply it.

Biases in Sampling

Now we're going to look at biases in sampling. There are a number of sampling biases, but we are going to focus on five, namely, selection bias, area bias, self-selection bias, leading question bias, and social desirability bias. These are the most common in a business setting.

Selection Bias

Selection bias is the most important, and the other biases can be considered related or even seen as subsets of this type of bias.

This type of bias exists when the sample is not representative because there is some kind of process taking place that makes sure the subjects or the items in the sample are special. Many other subjects or items are not included.

#An interesting story about selection bias is the one of Abraham Wald, who was a statistician. During World War II, the government reached out to him to ask him to improve the survival rate of US aircraft. Wald was smart, and the first thing he did was to look at the prior analyses that had been conducted. And he noticed that selection bias was taking place.
The previous investigators had been analyzing aircraft that survived and recommended that more armor should be added to the areas that had received the most damage, thereby increasing their protection. So, where the planes were most shot and torn up, new armor was mounted to protect those areas.

The result was that even more planes went down. The additional armor made the planes heavier, leading to them being less agile and slower. And the planes still returned with damage in the same areas.
The problem was that the investigators had based their conclusions on planes that had been damaged in areas that were clearly resilient. After all, they had taken damage in those areas and still returned to base.
Wald realized that what needed to be protected was the areas that had not taken damage and

were sensitive. Once armor was added to those areas, survivability increased. It's a very interesting example of using statistics in a highly intelligent way without even running an analysis. All he had to do was realize that this selection bias was in play and then he fixed it.

Area Bias

Area bias occurs when you try to generalize results from one area to another area, and this is especially problematic when attempting to cross cultures.

So, for example, you conduct marketing research in Europe and you automatically assume the same results will hold for the United States. Unfortunately, this doesn't take into account that a wide range of factors, including cultural and financial, could affect the validity of the results.

Self-Selection Bias

In self-selection bias, a person's decision to take part in a study could be correlated with traits they already have and which could affect the study, making the participants a non-representative sample.

This might sound complicated, but it's actually a lot simpler than it sounds. For example, if you were to set up a booth to ask people about their grooming habits, the people who respond are more likely to be people who like taking care of themselves and spend more time primping in the mornings. The problem is that you need to talk to both people who primp and also those who are less interested in grooming in the mornings for the sample to be representatives.

Leading Question Bias

Leading question bias is about how questions are phrased and asked, but also what the answer options are.

So, if you were to ask

Don't you think high school teachers are paid too little?

A) Yes, they should earn more.
B)No, they should not earn more.
C) No opinion.

Most people would answer A because of the way the question was phrased. Thus, with leading questions, you end up with biased results.

Social Desirability Bias

Social desirability bias occurs when people want to seem better than they are. For example, if you ask people in survey about how often they shower or how frequently they recycle, your data will be biased because no one wants to admit to doing something that is socially undesirable.

In other words, even if someone showers every 2 weeks, they're going to tell you they do it once a day or every 3 days or whatever they think is a more socially acceptable number. Whatever it is, it's rarely going to be the truth.

Sampling Bias in the Real World

The previous examples were all quite simple. However, the polling for the 2016 American Presidential Election is a good case where these sampling biases combined to affect the results. Another example is Brexit.

In both cases, the pollsters' results weren't that accurate. Most of the explanations of what happened revolved around biasing in sampling. There are all sorts of theories regarding what happened.

For example, the Pew Research Center stated the following:

One likely culprit is what pollsters refer to as nonresponse bias. This occurs when certain kinds of people systematically do not respond to surveys despite equal opportunity outreach to all parts of the electorate. We know that some groups—including the less educated voters who were a key demographic for Trump on Election Day—are consistently hard for pollsters to reach. It is possible that the frustration and anti-institutional feelings that drove the Trump campaign may also have aligned with an unwillingness to respond to polls.

Another theory was that there was self-selection in online polling, saying that people who tend to answer online polls were more likely to support a certain candidate over another. There was also the assumption that people who supported the other party wanted to avoid polls altogether.

It once again shows how statistics can also go wrong not because of the math or the models but due to factors outside of our control, namely, sampling biases.

This is similar to spurious correlations in a way, because statistics is an applied science and doesn't happen in a vacuum. If you don't have the right data, if you don't have the right theory, you will still come up with a set of numbers but they won't mean anything.

Lying with Inferential Statistics

So, while it might not be that easy to lie with inferential statistics, those of you who might have harbored the illusion that it's not possible at all will be disappointed because it can be done.

It happens in large part in research. When you test a hypothesis, you get a p-value, which you want to be below a certain threshold for the test to have statistical significance. Usually this threshold is 0.05.

There's a theory about the cult of the p-value that says there are a very large number of research papers out there with p-values suspiciously close to 0.05. Essentially, they're just below 0.05 so they can meet the condition of statistical significance. This might make the results significant, but only marginally so. The theory is that this is being done on purpose. In academia, the environment is very competitive and people have to publish or they'll lose their job. Thus, many people are under pressure to make their p-values look more significant than they might actually be.

One way to do this is to run multiple experiments until you get the results you want, and another way is to massage the data. In some cases, though, you might find research where the results are significant but the researcher's intent is not to deceive, but it could be that the model assumptions are not being met.

All models and statistics have some assumptions, and unfortunately there are many research papers out there where these assumptions are not being properly accounted for.

IN DEPTH: BAYESIAN VS. FREQUENTIST STATISTICS

Maybe you have heard of the term "Bayesian." There are many models that include the word "Bayes": "Naïve Bayes," "Bayesian networks," "Bayesian inference," and so on.

All these refer to a school of thought behind statistics. It all started with the British mathematician Reverend Thomas Bayes, who came up with this simple formula:

$$P(A|B) = \frac{P(B|A)P(A)}{P(B)}$$

This formula describes the probability of event A taking place, given that B has taken place as well. This was later developed further by Pierre-Simon Laplace and Sir Harold Jeffreys into what is now forming the foundations of Bayesian statistics.

One of the main ideas behind Bayesian statistics is that it is possible to incorporate prior knowledge about something into our analysis, be it a model or a significance test. On the other hand, frequentist statistics (which is the most popular statistical theory) do not accommodate that, neither do they allow it.

So, for example, let's say that you want to run some experiment to prove that ghosts exist. You have two hypotheses (ghosts exist or not). A Bayesian statistician can preassign a very small probability to the hypothesis that ghosts do not exist based on common sense. Hence, the experiment should find overwhelming evidence in favor of the ghost hypothesis before the test is significant. A frequentist doesn't have this choice.

Let's see another example. Frequentist statistics are formulated under the concept of an infinite number of experiments. For example, if you flip a fair coin a large number of times (thousands or more), then the actual probability of flipping heads will converge to 0.5.

However, how can this analogy work for events such as football games or elections? These events are unique. A game between two teams in a specific point in time is not going to be repeated. Even if it were, the parameters underlying it (e.g., how tired the players are or the members of a political party) might change. We can't perform an infinite number of these events. A Frequentist is in trouble in this case, but this is not a problem for a Bayesian.

In Bayesian statistics, probabilities express subjective beliefs of events happening, not repeated experiments.

Bayesian statistics have proven to be very useful and to also provide a theoretical framework for parts of machine learning. There are still many disagreements in the statistics community as to which theory is the best. In practice, frequentist statistics are used more often, but there are also many applications based on Bayesian statistics.

Once again, it's about finding the right tool for the job!

A Short Introduction
To Machine Learning
CHAPTER 12

A Short Introduction To Machine Learning

Machine learning has been defined in many ways by different researchers. The following are definitions from some of the most prominent researchers in the field:

Machine learning is programming computers to optimize a performance criterion using example data or past experience. —Ethem Alpaydin

The goal of machine learning is to develop methods that can automatically detect patterns in data, and then to use the uncovered patterns to predict future data or other outcomes of interest. —Kevin P. Murphy

The field of pattern recognition is concerned with the automatic discovery of regularities in data through the use of computer algorithms and with the use of these regularities to take actions. —Christopher M. Bishop

So, while these definitions are slightly different, but in one way or another, they involve algorithms that can learn from experience and data by identifying patterns or using other methods. They then use what they have learned to take action. Let's take a look at a simple example to gain a better understanding of how machine learning works. In Figure 11-1, I'm showing you a fictional dataset that consists of images of cats and dogs.

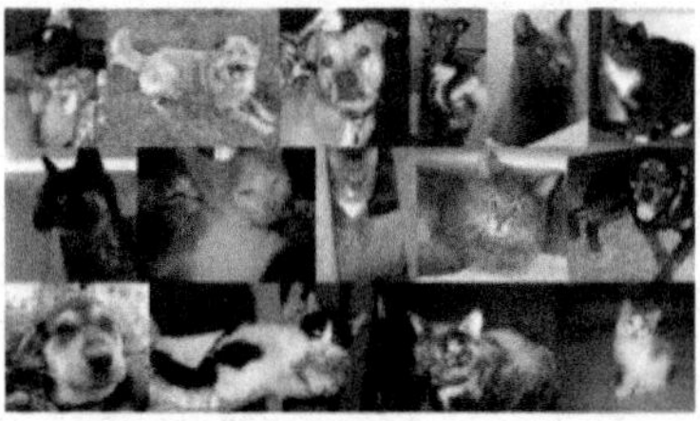

Figure 12-1. Classification example

If I ask you which images depict dogs and which ones cats, it is ridiculously easy to do. But how does it happen? First of all, your brain has been exposed to a huge number of images of cats and dogs, but also examples of those animals in real life.

You have trained yourself to be able to discriminate between these two and other animals through countless rounds of feedback from sources like your family, school, and TV. However, this whole process isn't quite as simple as it seems. Your brain has been optimized through thousands and thousands of years of evolution to make these associations easily. Even if you knew nothing about cats and dogs, your brain would quickly figure out that these two entities look like different animals. Your brain can aggregate these images very quickly and it immediately understands that while they are different, they all refer to the same species.

For a machine, though, this is much more difficult, which is why machine learning is so important because it's about imitating this process and replicating it within a machine.

The Main Advantage of Machine Learning

Learning from data is very easy for the human brain to do but difficult for a machine to do because it requires the right algorithms and lots of data to achieve.

However, what is easy for a machine is implementation and automation. Once you've got the algorithm, it's easy for a machine to go through thousands or even millions of images without experiencing any fatigue, which is impossible for a human brain to do.

It means you can create something very powerful with superhuman capabilities, even if we're talking about a narrow field of application, such as image classification. And this is exactly what makes machine learning and big data such a powerful combination.

Types of Machine Learning

Now, we're going to take a quick look at the different fields in machine learning (Table 7-1). The main fields in machine learning are supervised and unsupervised learning. Reinforcement learning has been gaining ground and related fields such as recommender systems can also be linked to machine learning, but they are more niche and not within the scope of this book.

Table 12-1. Types of machine learning

Name	Use
Supervised learning	Use a model *M* to predict target variable *Y* from input *X*.
Unsupervised learning	Find patterns in variable *X* (clustering is the most common example).
Reinforcement learning	Teach an agent how to optimize a reward function over the environment. For example, a video game AI can take 10 different actions, which need to be done as a response to the environment in order to maximize to reach a goal (e.g., maximize a score or beat a human player).
Active learning	Supervised learning with active feedback from a human.
Semi-supervised learning	Supervised learning, where some examples are unlabeled. For example, a dataset of 10000 images, where 1000 do not have a label, can be analyzed through semi-supervised learning techniques.
Recommender systems	Find a set of items to offer to a user that the user is likely to like (e.g., movies to watch, products to buy, songs to listen). Heavily related to supervised learning.

Supervised Learning

Supervised learning can be classified into classification and regression, which are both quite similar. In supervised learning, there is some form of supervision of the algorithm. We provide the algorithm with raw dataset, but then we also provide it with a target. The latter can be a single variable or multiple variables. Then, the algorithm attempts to understand how to match the input to the output. For example, you provide the algorithm with customer data and then it tries to determine if someone will make a purchase or not. The supervisor oversees what the algorithm is doing. Every time the algorithm makes a mistake, the supervisor tries to correct it. It's basically like the algorithm is learning under the guidance of a teacher.

Unsupervised Learning

Unsupervised learning, in the context of machine learning, usually refers to clustering. In this case, we provide the algorithm with raw data, but instead of providing a target, the algorithm is allowed to do its own thing essentially and identify patterns in the data provided. It tries to find any regularities that seem significant, but there is no supervision involved.

This type of learning is a very difficult problem because it's ill-defined and almost always requires a human to interpret usually toward the final stage of the pipeline. For example, the algorithm might identify patterns that are irrelevant to what you are trying to do, which is why you need to drill down into the results and try to define them a little better.

Supervised learning, on the other hand, is a bit easier because you can run an algorithm and you can immediately determine how it works. You can analyze customer data, for example, and predict retention rates with an 80% accuracy. This is what makes supervised learning one of the most popular fields in the machine learning family.

It's important to note that some the terms we are using such as classification, regression, and clustering are used in statistics as well as machine learning. However, even if the terminology refers to almost the same thing, there are still some differences.

In statistics, interpretability is important, whereas it is of little consequence in machine learning. Likewise, in machine learning, we are interested in the predictive performance of the algorithm, while in statistics this is important.

The terminology might seem a little confusing when comparing the terms from statistics to machine learning because there are some models like logistics regression models that are classification models and are treated as classification models within the context of machine learning. The differences are mainly the result of different histories to the fields, so don't be confused if you hear people with different backgrounds using these terms in slightly different ways.

A Closer Look at Supervised Learning

Supervised learning is broken down into classification and regression. The difference between the two is quite simple. In classification, we try to identify if something belongs in a specific category, while in regression we try to predict a real number.

An easy example of a classification model is one where we attempt to determine whether an email is spam or not. It's a task that's found in every introductory machine learning textbook. Another popular task is image recognition or object identification, such as "is this an image of an animal?" or "does this image contain a human?" or "where in this picture can you find human faces?".

Classification can also be about other things. Determining whether a stock will rise or fall is one such application, and it's usually referred to as binary classification because there are two categories—rising or falling. Another application is to determine whether someone will click on an ad or will the temperature rise above 0 degrees.

You can have multiple categories too in some problems. For example, if you want to predict elections, in most cases, you have more than two election parties. In that case, you might have four or five classes, with each class representing one of the political parties running in the election.

Regression, on the other hand, attempts to predict a real number. So, instead of asking whether the price of a stock will rise or fall, we attempt to determine what the price of the stock will be in 2 weeks. Or, if we are attempting to determine customer demand for a particular product, we could attempt to figure out what demand will be like in 5 days, for example. Maybe instead of attempting to understand if someone will click on an ad, we want to find out how many people will click on an ad—it might be a related problem but it's still a different problem.

Likewise with temperature. A vague idea of whether it will rise or not might not be sufficient for your needs, so you might attempt to determine what the exact temperature will be in 3 weeks.
These two types of problems—classification and regression—can be found in many fields and in many

different contexts.
It's important to note that the same problem can be tackled using different approaches. Let's say that we work for a hedge fund and we want to predict the price of stocks so we can make a nice profit.

This problem can be tackled using statistical forecasting, machine learning regression, or even classification with the latter attempting to determine the direction price will head in, that is, either up or down.

The performance ceiling—or the best performance you can get—for each approach, though, will be different. This can have different effects on your strategy, depending on what you want to achieve.
For example, you might first attempt to use a classification model to predict the price of stock. But you realize then that you'll only know whether the price will rise or fall. This doesn't lend itself well to straight trading, so you might consider spread betting as an alternative. However, you might decide to take the slightly more difficult approach of a regression model because the increased profits will make it worth your while.

The key is to understand that a problem is often not just a single problem but a series of other problems within your main problem. Think of it a bit like a LEGO model. Each model is a whole—a castle, a helicopter, a spaceship—but it's built from separate blocks. In this case, the problem is the castle made up of sub-problems or blocks.

It also pays off to try multiple approaches to determine which one is the most effective for your needs. Again, it's like one of those multi-model LEGO sets.

You can use the same bricks in different ways to achieve the outcome you need.

Except that, unlike with a LEGO set, you don't have instructions or even inspirational pictures to help you on your journey—you have to keep testing different assembly approaches until you end up with what you need.

However, if you have a creative data scientist around to help you, it'll be like having those LEGO instructions and pictures on hand, making life much easier.

It's also important to choose your battles wisely. If you find that a regression model will generate better performance, even if it's more difficult to do and wasn't your initial choice, it's still a good idea to switch to ensure better results.

A Better Understanding of Unsupervised Learning

Unsupervised learning is about learning patterns from data without any kind of guidance. The main application is clustering, which is an automated way of creating groups, like with the images in Figure 12-1.
So, you can feed a bunch of animal pictures into an unsupervised learning algorithm, and it could group them automatically into two categories (cats and dogs) without any additional feedback.

One of the most prominent uses for unsupervised learning algorithms in business is for customer segmentation. So, you feed the algorithm customer data, and it identifies patterns and segments your customer base accordingly.

Another application is anomaly detection, which some consider to be its own separate category because it doesn't use just unsupervised learning but also borrows some techniques from supervised learning. However, I've included it here because it's good to know that it exists.

Dimensionality reduction is another application which involves reducing a large number of variables into what are called "factors" or super variables. So, you can take 20 variables, for example, and group them under one factor. It's a little like clustering, but for variables. The main reason to do this is because it makes it easier to understand the data.

Examples of Clustering

As already stated, unsupervised learning and clustering are fundamentally very difficult problems, mainly because they are ill-defined. So, let's say we are given the objects in Figure 11-2 to cluster.

Figure 12-2. Clustering example

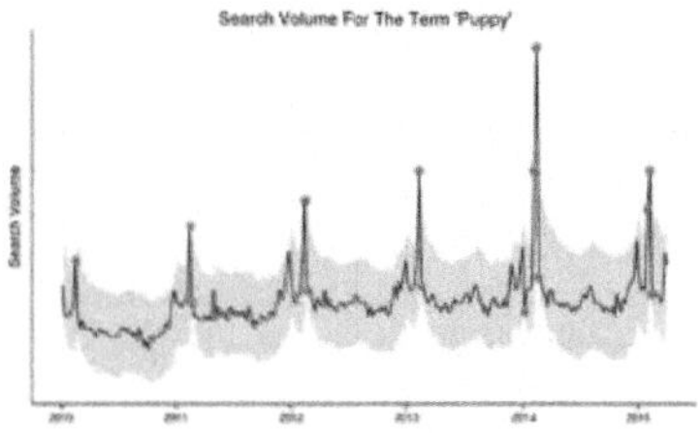

Figure 12-3. Anomaly detection example over a time series

The problem is that there are numerous approaches. You could cluster according to color. Or, you could cluster by type, namely, based on whether the object is a fruit or vegetable. Or maybe you want to cluster based on shape.

However, if you want to cluster, for example, based on color, this doesn't mean that the other approaches are wrong. All the patterns are valid. The question is whether they are useful, and the answer depends on what your goal is.
Thus, clustering algorithms attempt to identify these patterns, but sometimes the results aren't that useful or aren't relevant to what you need. It's why you always need a bit of experimentation before you can get it right. At the end of the day, though, if you know what you're doing and you try a few different algorithms, you will eventually find one that works.

Unsupervised learning has been around for decades so there are a wide range of very powerful algorithms that can identify patterns in data if they exist. However, it's important to keep in mind that just because you think objects should be clustered in a certain way doesn't mean the first algorithm you try will come up with the same result.

Examples of Anomaly Detection
Anomaly detection is about anomalous or unusual behavior in different contexts. Figure **12-3** is a time series, and by running an anomaly detection algorithm, we can see that the search volume for the term 'puppy' spikes every January.
How is this useful? Well, if you own a pet shop or if you run a dog shelter, you'll know when is the best time to match puppies with new families or to increase your puppy-related inventory.

Likewise, this kind of analysis is used for a wide range of applications. It can be used in retail for a wide range of products, or it can be used to analyze social media activity to understand whether people talk about particular subjects and if a topic has created a spike.

Anomaly detection is extensively used in cyber-security to detect hackers. So, if 99% of the traffic going to a server is normal and then you have 1% that is exhibiting anomalous behavior, anomaly detection algorithms will flag the suspicious behavior so action can be taken accordingly.

Examples of Dimensionality Reduction

In **Figure 12-4**, you can see a summary of the Big Five personality traits. It is one of the most successful theories in psychology.

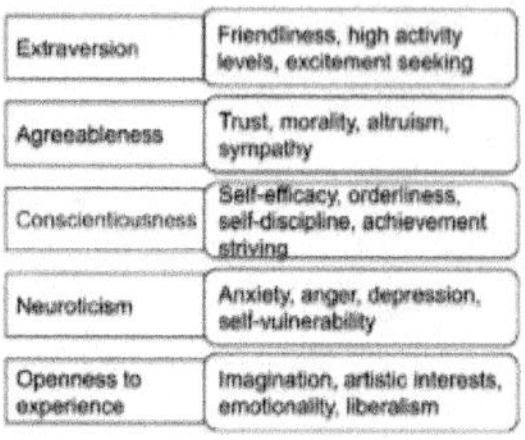

Figure 12-4. Summary of the Big Five personality traits

So, what does the Big Five personality theory have to do with dimensionality reduction? Well, this theory was derived by running factor analysis, one of the most prominent dimensionality reduction techniques.

This personality theory was the result of people answering a large number of questions in a questionnaire and then applying factor analysis to group these questions into five overall factors. As you can see, according to this theory, personality is broken down into

- Extraversion
- Agreeableness
- Conscientiousness
- Neuroticism
- Openness to experience

This is an excellent example of where dimensionality reduction can be used. It is also sometimes used in supervised learning because it can de-noise data, but this is more of a technical issue. However, it can also be used in any other context where you have a large number of variables.

For example, in my PhD thesis, I worked with GPS data from the training sessions of the Tottenham Hotspur football club. The GPS units we used collected over 100 different variables, which the sports science team found very difficult to interpret. So, I resorted to supervised principal component analysis and reduced them down to five or six factors that correlated with injury, which made the results much easier to understand.

As you can see, it can be applied to many things. There's nothing that says you can't do the same with user demographics or customer data and so on.

INTERPRETABLE MACHINE LEARNING

Machine learning has often been called a black box, and rightly so. Not only the algorithms can seem difficult to understand to the uninitiated, but also the algorithms are usually designed for performance, and predictive power, but not interpretability.
However, there is a new niche in machine learning that is set to change all that: interpretable machine learning. Interpretable machine learning is focused on coming up with techniques and methods in order to make machine learning models more transparent. For example, one such simple technique to use is called the "surrogate model" technique. A decision tree is fit on the predictions of a more complicated model (e.g., a deep neural network). The decision tree can be easily interpreted, even by someone who is not a data scientist, and can very quickly help you spot out the most important variables and how they interact. Two other more advanced techniques are LIME and Shapley value explanations. LIME stands for Local Interpretable Model-Agnostic Explanations and is a technique that can be used to explain any outcome. Shapley value explanation is a technique inspired by game theory,
which can be used to understand the importance of variables and how they interact within a model for it to reach a particular conclusion.

In Figure **12-5**, you can see how, for example, LIME can spot the most important words for text classifier. The text classifier is trying to discriminate between posts that are talking about atheism and posts that are talking about Christianity. The algorithm can produce a list of importance of the different words, which are then highlighted in the text.
Interpretable machine learning methods will become more and more important as algorithms are being used more and more often to make decisions in all parts of our lives. You can read more at Data Scientist Website.

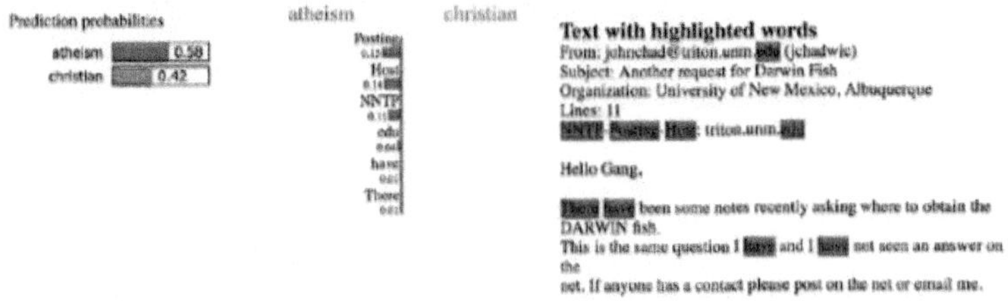

Figure 12-5. Example of how LIME can examine feature importance

CHAPTER 13

The Present And Future Of AI

The Present And Future Of AI

Exploring the Realm of Artificial Intelligence

Artificial Intelligence (AI) is a field that has captivated our imagination and transformed numerous aspects of our lives. It is a term often thrown around, but what exactly does it mean? In this chapter, we will delve into the various areas of AI, shed light on the difference between narrow and general AI, and touch upon the intriguing concept of Generative AI.

Understanding the Different Areas of AI

Artificial Intelligence encompasses a wide range of applications and techniques. Let's explore some of the key areas:

Machine Learning: This branch of AI focuses on enabling computers to learn and improve from experience without being explicitly programmed. Machine learning algorithms analyse vast amounts of data, recognize patterns, and make predictions or decisions based on this learning. It is widely used in tasks such as image and speech recognition, recommendation systems, and fraud detection.

Natural Language Processing (NLP): NLP enables computers to understand, interpret, and generate human language. It involves tasks like sentiment analysis, machine translation, question-answering systems, and chatbots. NLP has revolutionised how we interact with technology, making it more intuitive and human-like.

Computer Vision: Computer vision enables computers to interpret and understand visual information from images or videos. It encompasses tasks such as object recognition, image classification, and facial recognition. Computer vision has found applications in areas like autonomous vehicles, surveillance systems, and medical diagnostics.

Robotics: Robotics combines AI with mechanical engineering to create intelligent machines that can perceive and interact with the physical world. Robots can perform complex tasks in various industries, including manufacturing, healthcare, and exploration. They have the potential to enhance efficiency, productivity, and safety in many fields.

Narrow AI vs. General AI

When we talk about AI, it's important to distinguish between narrow AI and general AI.

Narrow AI, also known as weak AI, refers to systems designed to perform specific tasks. These systems excel in their predefined domains but lack the ability to generalise beyond them.
Examples include voice assistants like Siri or Alexa, autonomous vehicles, and recommendation algorithms. Narrow AI is highly specialised and focused, offering practical solutions but with limited scope.

On the other hand, general AI, also called strong AI or artificial general intelligence (AGI), refers to systems that possess human-like intelligence and can perform any intellectual task that a human being can do. General AI would exhibit reasoning, understanding, and problem-solving abilities across a wide range of domains. However, creating true general AI remains a complex and ongoing challenge, with researchers pushing the boundaries of what's possible.

Generative AI: Creating Something from Nothing

Within the realm of AI, one particularly fascinating area is Generative AI. While traditional AI systems learn from existing data to generate insights or predictions, Generative AI takes a step further by creating original content.

Generative AI employs techniques such as Generative Adversarial Networks (GANs) or Variational Autoencoders (VAEs) to generate new and realistic data. For example, GANs can create lifelike images, mimic an artist's style, or generate synthetic voices. These systems are trained on vast datasets and learn to generate novel content that closely resembles the training data.

Generative AI has applications in various fields, including art, design, entertainment, and even drug discovery. It opens up exciting possibilities for creativity and innovation, enabling machines to produce content that was once the sole domain of human beings.

Generative Artificial Intelligence (AI) is a fascinating area that brings machines closer to the realm of creativity and imagination. Unlike traditional AI systems that rely on analysing existing data, generative AI goes a step further by enabling machines to create original content. This innovative field utilises techniques such as Generative Adversarial Networks (GANs) or Variational Autoencoders (VAEs) to generate new and realistic data, such as images, music, or even text.

Imagine a scenario where you want an AI system to create a piece of artwork in the style of a renowned painter. Generative AI can make that happen. By training a GAN on a vast dataset of the painter's works, the system learns to capture the unique style, brushstrokes, and colour palettes. It can then generate new images that closely resemble the artistic style of the painter, producing stunning and original pieces of art. This capability opens up new horizons for artistic expression, as machines can now contribute their own creative output alongside human artists.

Generative AI also finds applications in the world of music. By training AI models on a diverse range of musical compositions, the system can learn the patterns, harmonies, and melodies of different genres. It can then compose new music pieces that possess similar characteristics, demonstrating the ability to create original compositions in the style of famous composers or even generating unique and innovative musical pieces that push the boundaries of what we consider "traditional" music.. Another fascinating aspect of generative AI is its potential to transform the written word. AI models trained on vast amounts of text data can learn the structure, grammar, and vocabulary of various languages. They can then generate text that mimics the style and tone of different authors or even create entirely new narratives. For instance, an AI-powered chatbot can engage in conversations that are not only coherent and contextually relevant but also demonstrate a unique personality, enhancing the user experience and providing more natural interactions.

Generative AI is not limited to the realm of art and creativity alone. It has the potential to revolutionise fields such as design, architecture, and product development. By training AI models on vast collections of designs, blueprints, and architectural plans, generative AI can create new and innovative designs that meet specific criteria and constraints. This technology empowers designers and architects to explore a vast range of possibilities, generate novel ideas, and push the boundaries of what is considered possible.

However, generative AI also raises important questions and challenges. As AI systems become more proficient at generating realistic content, issues surrounding copyright, ethics, and authenticity emerge. Determining the ownership and originality of AI-generated works poses legal and ethical challenges that need to be addressed.

In conclusion, generative AI is an exciting frontier that pushes the boundaries of what machines can achieve in terms of creativity and imagination. By training AI models on vast datasets and leveraging advanced algorithms, machines can generate original content, from artwork and music to text and designs. This technology opens up new avenues for collaboration between humans and machines, enriching artistic expression, enabling innovative designs, and transforming various industries. As generative AI continues to evolve, it will undoubtedly shape our future and redefine our understanding of creativity.

Image Recognition

Artificial Intelligence (AI) has made remarkable advancements in various domains, and one area that has particularly caught the attention of researchers and technology enthusiasts is image recognition. Image recognition is the process by which machines can analyse and interpret visual data, such as photographs or videos, and understand the objects, scenes, or patterns within them. This remarkable capability has opened up a plethora of possibilities and has transformed numerous industries.

At the heart of image recognition lies the field of computer vision, which combines AI algorithms with the ability to perceive and understand visual information. Using deep learning techniques, machines can learn to recognize objects, people, and even subtle details within images. This has paved the way for numerous practical applications, revolutionising fields such as healthcare, security, automotive, and e-commerce.

In healthcare, image recognition has proven to be a game-changer. Medical professionals can utilise AI-powered systems to analyse medical images, such as X-rays, CT scans, and MRIs, to identify diseases, tumours, or anomalies with greater accuracy. This not only saves time but also enhances the diagnostic capabilities, leading to better patient outcomes. Moreover, AI-based image recognition systems can assist in the early detection of diseases like cancer, improving the chances of successful treatment.

The impact of image recognition is also evident in the realm of security and surveillance. Advanced video analytics systems can monitor live video feeds, automatically detecting and alerting authorities about suspicious activities or objects in real-time. This technology can aid in the prevention of crimes, assist in tracking missing persons, and enhance the overall security infrastructure of public spaces. With AI-powered image recognition, security personnel can efficiently process and analyse vast amounts of visual data, ensuring a safer environment for everyone.

Another exciting application of image recognition is seen in the automotive industry, particularly in the development of autonomous vehicles. AI-powered cameras and sensors enable these vehicles to identify and recognize various objects and road conditions, making crucial decisions to ensure safe navigation. From detecting pedestrians and other vehicles to interpreting traffic signs and signals, image recognition plays a vital role in the perception and decision-making capabilities of self-driving cars.

In the world of e-commerce, image recognition has transformed the way we shop online. With the rise of mobile shopping, AI-powered apps can now recognize products from images taken by users, enabling seamless product searches and recommendations. This technology allows users to simply snap a photo of an item they like and instantly find similar products or make a purchase. This not only enhances the user experience but also enables businesses to provide personalised and targeted recommendations, ultimately driving sales.

The advancements in image recognition owe much to the power of deep learning algorithms, particularly Convolutional Neural Networks (CNNs). These networks are designed to mimic the functioning of the human visual system, with multiple layers of neurons processing and analysing visual data at increasing levels of complexity. By training CNNs on massive datasets containing labelled images, they learn to extract meaningful features and patterns, enabling accurate and efficient image recognition.

In conclusion, image recognition powered by AI has revolutionised various industries, ranging from healthcare and security to automotive and e-commerce. The ability of machines to analyse and interpret visual data has opened up endless possibilities, enhancing diagnostics, improving security, enabling autonomous vehicles, and transforming online shopping experiences. As AI continues to advance, we can expect image recognition to become even more sophisticated, unlocking new realms of applications and redefining the way we perceive and interact with the visual world.

Extended Reality & AI

Extended Reality (XR) is an exciting and transformative technology that blurs the line between the physical and digital worlds, offering immersive experiences that captivate our senses. XR encompasses three main categories: Augmented Reality (AR), Virtual Reality (VR), and Mixed Reality (MR). Each of these technologies has its unique characteristics and applications, and when combined with the power of Artificial Intelligence (AI), they can revolutionise various aspects of our lives.

Augmented Reality (AR) brings digital elements into the real world, overlaying computer-generated images, text, or animations onto our physical environment. AR is commonly experienced through smartphones or smart glasses, enabling users to see digital information integrated seamlessly into their surroundings. For instance, AR navigation apps can display directions on the street while looking through a phone's camera, or AR gaming apps can project virtual characters in the real world, creating interactive and engaging experiences. The impact of AI on AR is profound. AI algorithms can analyse real-time data from sensors and cameras, recognize objects, and identify environments, allowing AR applications to understand the context and respond intelligently. This opens up possibilities for more interactive and personalised AR experiences, such as virtual shopping assistants that recommend products based on user preferences or language translation apps that instantly translate foreign signs.

Virtual Reality (VR) transports users to entirely computer-generated environments, immersing them in virtual worlds through headsets or goggles. VR creates a sense of presence, making users feel as if they are physically present in the digital environment. This technology has found applications in various industries, such as gaming, education, training, and therapy. In gaming, VR offers unparalleled levels of immersion, allowing players to interact with virtual worlds using their movements and gestures. AI plays a significant role in enhancing VR experiences. AI-powered algorithms can track users' movements and gestures, enabling more realistic and responsive interactions in virtual environments. Moreover, AI can generate dynamic content in VR, such as realistic characters that behave intelligently and adapt to users' actions, making the experiences more lifelike and engaging.

Mixed Reality (MR) is a blend of both AR and VR, where digital objects are integrated into the real world and interact with it in real-time. MR allows users to see and manipulate virtual objects as if they were physically present, combining the best of both worlds. Microsoft's HoloLens is a popular example of MR technology. The impact of AI on MR is significant, as AI algorithms can understand the spatial context of the real world, enabling virtual objects to interact intelligently with physical surroundings. This integration of AI with MR has implications across industries, from design and engineering, where engineers can visualise and interact with 3D models in real-time, to healthcare, where surgeons can use MR to visualise medical data during procedures, enhancing precision and efficiency.

The fusion of XR and AI holds enormous potential and is poised to revolutionise various sectors. In the education sector, XR technologies can provide immersive and interactive learning experiences, making complex subjects more engaging and understandable. AI-powered virtual tutors can adapt to individual learning styles, offering personalised guidance and feedback to students. In healthcare, XR combined with AI can improve patient care and training for medical professionals. Surgeons can practise complex procedures in virtual simulations, reducing the risk of errors in real-life operations. Additionally, AI algorithms can analyse medical data and assist in diagnosing diseases, enabling faster and more accurate treatments.

The impact of XR and AI is also felt in the business world. XR technologies enable remote collaboration, with teams from different locations working together as if they were in the same room, enhancing productivity and efficiency. AI-driven analytics in XR can provide valuable insights and data visualisation, helping businesses make informed decisions and optimise processes.

Conclusion

In this chapter, we have explored the fascinating world of Artificial Intelligence (AI) and its ever-expanding applications. From narrow AI systems that excel in specific tasks to the ambitious pursuit of general AI, we have witnessed the transformative power of AI in various domains. AI has revolutionised industries such as healthcare, finance, transportation, and entertainment, enhancing efficiency, improving decision-making, and unlocking new possibilities. As AI continues to evolve and push boundaries, it holds the promise of shaping the future in profound ways. The integration of AI with emerging technologies like Extended Reality (XR), Robotics, and Internet of Things (IoT) will further amplify its impact, creating intelligent and interconnected systems that enhance our daily lives. However, the future of AI also poses ethical considerations, such as ensuring transparency, fairness, and accountability in AI systems. As we move forward, it is crucial to foster responsible AI development, with a focus on human-centred design and the alignment of AI advancements with societal values. By embracing AI's potential while addressing its challenges, we can harness its power to drive innovation, solve complex problems, and create a future where AI augments human capabilities and leads to a more prosperous and inclusive society.

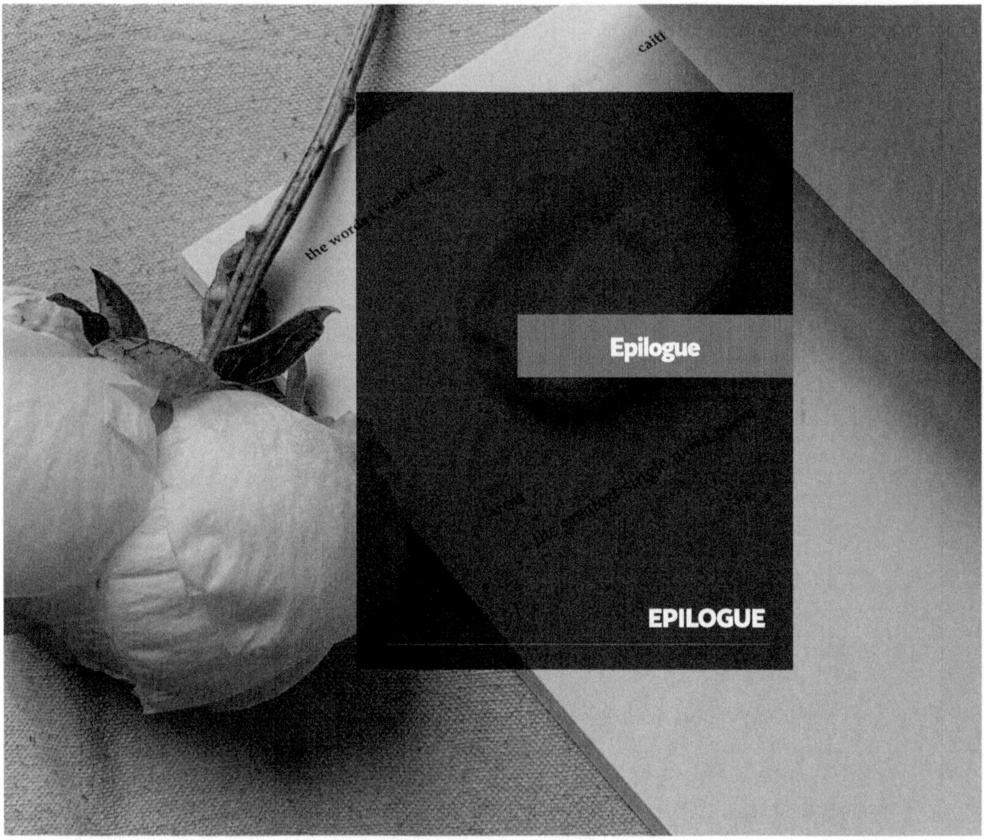
Epilogue
EPILOGUE

EPILOGUE

Data Science Rules the World

Data is being created and consumed at an unprecedented scale. Data science is progressing even faster, further speeding up the rate of data creation and consumption.

It is clear that data science is expanding both vertically and horizontally across all industries and layers of society. The companies that are the first to adopt the best practices will gain a significant advantage. The rest might just perish. The situation is to a large extent equivalent to a paradigm shift in the means of production, like the one that was experienced through the industrial revolution, making many people talk about a fourth industrial revolution.

The history of data science is not linear. Its roots are in mathematics and philosophy, in the vision of the AI fathers to create a thinking machine, in computational intelligence and data mining, and in many other fields and ideas as to how we can extrapolate from a simple piece of information to describe a universe of concepts. After centuries, the science, engineering, and availability in data and computing power have created a perfect storm, and this storm is only going to get stronger.

I hope this book provided you with enough insights as to how data science can be applied in business. Data management, data strategy, choosing the right algorithms, hiring data scientists, and having the right culture all these factors are interleaved when a company attempts to extract insights from data. Doing data science is more complicated than simply hiring a data scientist, but, at the same time, it can be much easier than creating a novel algorithm from scratch.

Being aware of these facts is the first step toward building a data-centric organization. This book has provided you with enough material, examples, and case studies to be aware of the opportunities, but also the pitfalls that may arise. Maybe you've not absorbed all the lessons now, but that's fine. Not everything might resonate at first instance. After you start working with data, you will revisit some of the chapters, and then they will make more sense, as you will be able to attach your experiences to the teachings inside this book.

What's important is that you've decided to stay and be part of this revolution by learning how to use data science in your company.

I wish you success on this journey.

Frameworks & Workbook

FRAMEWORKS & WORKBOOK

Data Science Project Assessment Questionnaire.pdf

HDS_Questionaire.pdf

Data Strategy Canvas.pdf

Pragmatic Data Strategy V2.pdf

DS10 Questionnaire.pdf

Simplified Project Management .pdf

The quick data privacy and cybersecurity accountability checklist.pdf

The Data Maturity Assessment framework.pdf

The lean AI ethics framework.pdf

The Data Product Framework for Startups.pdf

Tokenomics Framework Questionnaire.pdf

The-new-solution-adoption-questionnaire.pdf

The quick data privacy and cybersecurity accountability checklist.pdf

THE DATA-DRIVEN FUTURE:

UNLEASHING THE POWER OF AI AND EXPONENTIAL TECHNOLOGIES

Unleash the Power of AI and Exponential Technologies in "The Data-Driven Future." This accessible and engaging book breaks down complex concepts for non-technical readers, offering a clear understanding of how AI and data are revolutionizing industries and driving innovation. Discover how AI technologies, such as machine learning and deep neural networks, are transforming businesses and providing practical applications through real-world examples. Learn how to leverage data as the lifeblood of modern enterprises, optimize operations, and deliver personalized customer experiences. With practical frameworks and ethical considerations, this book equips you with the knowledge and tools to navigate the data-driven future and unlock new opportunities for growth.

Decision Makers

Printed in Great Britain
by Amazon

32613498R00116